MULTICOOKER
EVERYTHING

DELICIOUS RECIPES FOR YOUR MULTICOOKER,
PRESSURE COOKER OR INSTANT POT®

RICARDO

Appetite by Random House® and colophon are registered trademarks of Penguin Random House LLC.

Library and Archives Canada Cataloguing in Publication is available upon request.

ISBN: 9780525612469
eBook ISBN: 9780525612476

THE RICARDO TEAM
Author: Ricardo
Recipe Development: Nicolas Cadrin, Isabelle Deschamps Plante, Étienne Marquis, Laurence Viens
Recipe Development Contributor: Kareen Grondin
Recipe Tester: Danielle Bessette
Content Director: Maude Bourcier-Bouchard
Art Director: Cristine Berthiaume, Caroline Blanchette
Photographers: Sophie Carrière, page 46. Maude Chauvin, pages 77, 98. David de Stefano, pages 13, 14, 17, 20, 34, 39, 44, 47, 76, 79, 84, 87, 88, 89, 100, 106. Christian Lacroix, pages 18, 21, 32, 42, 45, 59, 62, 80, 81, 85, 90, 102, 104. Mathieu Lévesque, page 101. Jean-Michel Poirier, pages 3, 5, 6, 7, 8, 10-11, 12, 16, 24, 26-27, 28, 29, 30, 31, 36, 38, 40, 41, 52, 54-55, 56, 58, 60-61, 63, 64, 65, 66, 67, 68, 71, 72, 74-75, 78, 82, 92, 96, 99, 103, 105, 108.
Designers: Geneviève Larocque, Jean-Michel Poirier, Olivier Savoie
Design Contributors: Audrey Boivin, Lydia Moscato, Caroline Nault, Sylvain Riel, Nataly Simard
Graphic Artist: Michèle Hénen
Editors: Marie-Pier Gagnon, Charline-Ève Pilon, Annie St-Amour
Translation: Joanna Fox
Translation Revision: Michelle Diamond, Jane Jackel
Project Manager - Kitchen: Eve Marchand
Production Coordinator: Marisol Moquin Laferrière

President and Editorial Director: Brigitte Coutu
General Manager: Mireille Arteau
Vice-President Communications and Brand Image: Nathalie Carbonneau

ricardocuisine.com

Additional design: Dylan Browne

Printed in China

Published in Canada by Appetite by Random House®, a division of Penguin Random House Canada Limited.

10 9 8 7 6 5 4 3 2 1

appetite
by RANDOM HOUSE

Penguin
Random House
Canada

mediterranean-inspired
chicken (page 51)

pulled bbq beef with beer
(page 60)

CONTENTS

CELEBRATING
THE MULTICOOKER

Some say the pressure cooker has changed their lives, and we absolutely agree! This appliance is probably the one that saves us the most time out of all the appliances in our kitchen. But its advantages go beyond simply the speed at which we can make recipes—because the pressure cooker also retains nutrients, enhances flavors, makes food tender and even saves energy. In short, it helps simplify the act of cooking.

In this book, we share our best recipes for the electric pressure cooker. In these pages, you'll discover our favorite recipes—tried, tested and retested so that they all guarantee kitchen success—that show off the versatility and performance of this incredible appliance. We've divided the book into chapters that cover the different types of dishes that work well using the pressure cooker—soups and broths, vegetables, meat, legumes and grains, and sauces and stews—and included a chapter for breakfasts and sweets too. Are you ready to turn up the pressure?

MULTICOOKER 101

Are you excited to discover all the features of the pressure cooker? Here's a brief overview of how this electrical appliance works, as well as some pro tips on how to best use it and an explanation of the three stages that make up the cooking time of each recipe.

The recipes included in this book have all been tested with the RICARDO-brand pressure cooker, and also pressure cookers from brands Instant Pot, Breville and Starfrit. The RICARDO version of the pressure cooker is equipped with pre-programmed cooking functions, which may not be the same as those of another brand. However, all pressure cookers work in the same way: cooking using pressure.

In the case of the RICARDO pressure cooker, the pre-programmable functions Meat, Poultry, Bean, Root vegetable and Soup work at high pressure (60 kPa), while the manually adjustable function allows you to adjust the pressure level (Low or High) as well as the cooking time.

If your pressure cooker has the same modes for pre-programmed cooking as the RICARDO brand, you can select those as noted in the recipes. However, some adjustments to timing may be necessary, as the pressure may vary from one brand or model to the other (check the instruction manual that came with your appliance for suggested cooking times).

If you don't have the pre-programmable functions, or you're not sure how yours compares, set the pressure level and the cooking time of your pressure cooker manually. You will then just have to set it to High pressure (or as indicated in the recipe) and enter the cooking time.

The Sauté function, which is used to sauté vegetables and brown meat, can be used without a lid, as this function has no pressure (just like the Steam and Yogurt functions).

 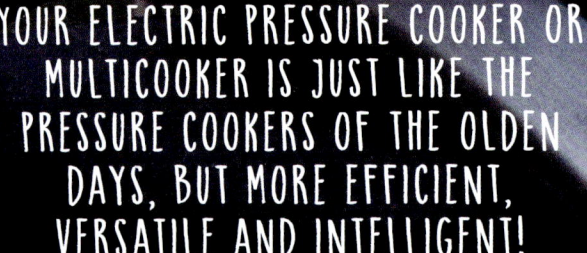

YOUR ELECTRIC PRESSURE COOKER OR MULTICOOKER IS JUST LIKE THE PRESSURE COOKERS OF THE OLDEN DAYS, BUT MORE EFFICIENT, VERSATILE AND INTELLIGENT!

WHAT IS IT?

Imagine the pressure cooker as a big pot where all you have to do is add the food, close the lid and press a button. Except that the cooking time is about two to three times faster! That speed is what makes this appliance use less energy overall than a stovetop, and save more of your own energy on weeknights. As a bonus, the food comes out full of flavor and packed with vitamins and minerals—since pressure cooking promotes the preservation of nutrients.

HOW DOES IT WORK?

The principle is simple: the pressure inside the cooker raises the temperature. Trapping the pressure—thanks to a hermetic lid—creates the heat that allows food to cook quickly.

IS IT SAFE?

The pressure cooker is equipped with a steam calibration system that releases excess steam (which means the pressure cannot get too high). If, however, it were to reach a critical level, the appliance would stop automatically.

COOKING TIME EXPLAINED

With the pressure cooker, the cooking time is divided into three stages that correspond to the pressurization, the pressure cooking and depressurization. These three stages subdivide the cooking time of each recipe in this book.

1. Pressurization

At this first stage, pressure builds up inside the pressure cooker. Pressurization time varies between 5 and 20 minutes, depending on the quantity and type of food being cooked and the temperature required to cook it.

2. Pressure cooking

This is the active cooking time, when the food is cooking. Once the pressure cooker is fully pressurized, it will switch automatically to active cooking, and the cooking time displayed on your appliance will start to count down.

3. Depressurization

After cooking, the pressure cooker needs to depressurize before you can remove the lid. Natural depressurization is when the appliance gently cools automatically; this takes about 15 minutes. You can accelerate the depressurization manually by turning the release valve to the position indicated on the lid (always do this while wearing an oven mitt or by using tongs, as the steam that comes out will be very hot). Proteins react differently to this sudden drop in pressure, which could affect their texture, so it is recommended that for meat, you always let your pressure cooker depressurize naturally. All the recipes indicate the depressurization type to follow, so there's no need to worry!

THREE PRO TIPS FOR YOUR MULTICOOKER

1. Respect the amount of liquid

Without a sufficient amount of liquid to create steam, the pressure cooker can't build enough pressure, and the food can't cook properly because of the absence of this pressure. So be mindful of carefully following the recipe recommendations for the amount of liquid to use. On the flip side, when there is too much liquid, a sauce can become diluted and will then have to be reduced further before serving. In general, it takes 1 ½ cups (375 ml) liquid (water, broth, juice, etc.).

2. Be mindful about increasing recipes

If you want to scale the recipe so it makes more, you must be careful not to fill the container too full or beyond the recommended maximum level. And watch out especially for adding too much of foods that contain starch, such as potatoes, rice, grains, legumes and pasta, as they expand with heat and the container of your pressure cooker could overflow.

3. Save time

To accelerate the heating of water (if the recipe requires it), you can warm it in the microwave first before adding it to the container.

Tom Kha-style chicken and coconut milk soup (page 23)

COCONUT MILK MAKES THIS SOUP
ULTRA-CREAMY. A PERFECT
MEAL FOR COLD DAYS!

SOUPS & BROTHS

Vegetable, chicken, beef, pork or seafood: Homemade broths are always better than store-bought ones. And with the pressure cooker, they take even less time to prepare and have a more concentrated flavor. Plus, they freeze well. The basic broth recipes in this chapter are all then paired with soups, so you can prepare a variety of delicious options that are sure to make everyone at the table happy. Certain dishes work perfectly in the pressure cooker, and soups are definitely one of them. Which one will you choose to start?

VEGETABLE BROTH

2	carrots, cut into pieces	2	sprigs thyme
2	stalks celery, cut into pieces	2	bay leaves
1	onion, halved	2 tsp	salt
1	tomato, quartered	½ tsp	black peppercorns
1	leek, cut into pieces	½ tsp	coriander seeds
10 cups	(2.5 L) water		

With the rack in the middle position, preheat the oven to broil. On a non-stick or foil-lined baking sheet, arrange the vegetables in an even layer. Bake for 15 minutes or until the vegetables are golden. Place the vegetables in the container of your pressure cooker.

Add the remaining ingredients. Secure the lid and select the Soup function (or set to High pressure). Set the cooking time to 25 minutes.

When ready, let your pressure cooker depressurize naturally (about 15 minutes), then remove the lid. Strain the broth through a sieve, then compost the vegetables, herbs and spices. The broth will keep for up to 5 days in the refrigerator or for up to 6 months in the freezer.

NOTE *Vegetable broth is perfect for making our meatless spaghetti sauce (recipe p. 99), veggie chili with black beans (recipe p. 112) or minestrone with winter vegetables (recipe p. 26).*

PREPARATION 30 MIN	**PRESSURE COOKING** 25 MIN	**MAKES** 10 CUPS (2.5 L)
PRESSURIZATION 20 MIN	**DEPRESSURIZATION** 15 MIN	**FREEZES** YES

IS YOUR BROTH ALREADY HOT?
YOU'LL SAVE 5 MINUTES OF
PRESSURIZATION TIME WHEN
YOU START WITH HOT BROTH.

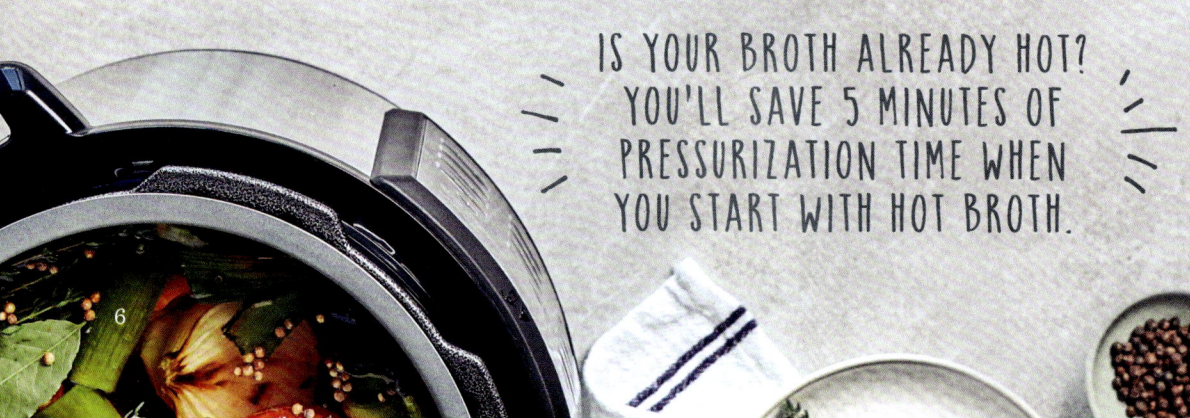

PORK BROTH

2	onions, halved
2	carrots, cut into pieces
2	stalks celery, cut into pieces
10 cups	(2.5 L) water
1 tbsp	black peppercorns

FOR MEATBALL STEW BROTH, ADD:

6	pork shank slices
2	bay leaves
2	cloves
2 tsp	salt

FOR SOY GARLIC BROTH, ADD:

1½ lb	(675 g) baby back pork ribs, cut into 4 pieces with 3 ribs each, soaked in water 1 hour, then rinsed and drained (see note)
4	green onions, cut into pieces
1	piece fresh ginger 2 inches (5 cm) long, washed and sliced
4	garlic cloves, peeled
¼ cup	(60 ml) soy sauce

Preheat the container of your pressure cooker on the Sauté function for 2 minutes. Brown the onions.

Add the remaining ingredients. Secure the lid and select the Soup function (or set to High pressure). Set the cooking time to 45 minutes.

When ready, let your pressure cooker depressurize naturally (about 15 minutes), then remove the lid. Skim as needed. Remove the pork shank or ribs. Remove the pork shank meat from the bones and remove the fat—set the meat aside. Keep the pieces of ribs intact (see note). Strain the broth through a sieve, then compost the bones, vegetables and spices. Let cool. Cover and refrigerate to allow the fat to rise to the surface and solidify, if desired. Degrease the cooled broth before use or freezing. The broth will keep for up to 5 days in the refrigerator or for up to 6 months in the freezer.

NOTES *Since it is not possible to skim during cooking, soaking the ribs in water beforehand removes most of the blood and impurities from the meat.*

The broth with the pork shank meat is perfect for making the meatball stew (recipe p. 123), and the one with the ribs is perfect for making pork soup with cabbage and potatoes (recipe p. 17).

PREPARATION 30 MIN	**PRESSURE COOKING** 45 MIN	**MAKES** 10 CUPS (2.5 L), APPROX.
PRESSURIZATION 25 MIN	**DEPRESSURIZATION** 15 MIN	**FREEZES** YES

CHICKEN BROTH

4	whole chicken legs (see note)
2	carrots, cut into pieces
2	stalks celery, cut into pieces
1	onion, quartered
1	leek, green part only, cut into pieces
2	garlic cloves, peeled
10 cups	(2.5 L) water
2 tsp	salt
1 tsp	black peppercorns
2	sprigs thyme (optional)
	A few sprigs parsley (optional)

Place all the ingredients in the container of your pressure cooker. Secure the lid and select the Soup function (or set to High pressure). Set the cooking time to 30 minutes.

When ready, let your pressure cooker depressurize naturally (about 15 minutes), then remove the lid. Remove the meat from the chicken bones and remove the fat—set aside (see note). Strain the broth through a sieve, then compost the bones, vegetables and herbs. Let the broth cool. Cover and refrigerate to allow the fat to rise to the surface and solidify, if desired. Degrease the cooled broth before use or freezing. The broth will keep for up to 5 days in the refrigerator or for up to 6 months in the freezer.

NOTES *You can use chicken legs or 1½ lb (675 g) chicken carcass. To make a turkey broth, use a big turkey leg. Set the cooking time to 40 minutes.*

Both the broth and the reserved cooked chicken are perfect for making chicken noodle soup with carrot juice (recipe p. 18).

PREPARATION	**PRESSURE COOKING**	**MAKES**
15 MIN	30 MIN	10 CUPS (2.5 L)
PRESSURIZATION	**DEPRESSURIZATION**	**FREEZES**
30 MIN	15 MIN	YES

BEEF BROTH

3 lb	(1.4 kg) beef marrow bones
2	onions, unpeeled, washed and halved
2	carrots, cut into pieces
2	large garlic cloves, peeled
10 cups	(2.5 L) water
2 tsp	salt
1 tsp	black peppercorns

FOR PHO BEEF BROTH, ADD:

2	pieces fresh unpeeled ginger 2 inches (5 cm) long, washed and halved lengthwise
1 tbsp	coriander seeds
1 tbsp	fennel seeds
1	clove
1	cinnamon stick about 1½ inches (4 cm) long
½	star anise

With the rack in the middle position, preheat the oven to 500°F (260°C). On a baking sheet, spread out the beef bones, onions, carrots and garlic (and ginger if making pho beef broth). Bake for 30 minutes or until the bones are well browned. Place the bones and vegetables in the container of your pressure cooker.

Add the remaining ingredients. Secure the lid and select the Soup function (or set to High pressure). Set the cooking time to 45 minutes.

When ready, let your pressure cooker depressurize naturally (about 15 minutes), then remove the lid. Strain the broth through a sieve, then compost the bones, vegetables and spices. Let cool. Cover and refrigerate to allow the fat to rise to the surface and solidify, if desired. Degrease the cooled broth before use or freezing. The broth will keep for up to 5 days in the refrigerator or for up to 6 months in the freezer.

NOTE *Beef broth is perfect for making beef bourguignon (recipe p. 120), beef with cherry tomatoes (recipe p. 52) or beef Stroganoff (recipe p. 116). Pho beef broth is perfect for preparing beef pho-style soup (recipe p. 14).*

PREPARATION	PRESSURE COOKING	MAKES
45 MIN	45 MIN	10 CUPS (2.5 L)

PRESSURIZATION	DEPRESSURIZATION	FREEZES
20 MIN	15 MIN	YES

SEAFOOD BROTH

1 lb	(450 g) seafood shells (lobster, crab and/or shrimp) or fish heads and carcasses, rinsed and drained
10 cups	(2.5 L) water
½ cup	(125 ml) white wine
	Fronds and stalks 1 fennel bulb, cut into pieces
2	stalks celery, cut into pieces
1	small leek, cut into pieces
¼ cup	(10 g) parsley sprigs
1 tbsp	(15 ml) tomato paste
2 tsp	salt
1 tsp	black peppercorns
1 tsp	fennel seeds

Place all the ingredients in the container of your pressure cooker. Secure the lid and select the Soup function (or set to High pressure). Set the cooking time to 15 minutes.

When ready, let your pressure cooker depressurize naturally (about 15 minutes), then remove the lid. Strain the broth through a fine sieve, then compost the shells, vegetables and spices. Adjust the seasoning. The broth will keep for up to 5 days in the refrigerator or for up to 6 months in the freezer.

NOTE *This broth is perfect for making shrimp and corn chowder (recipe p. 13).*

PREPARATION	PRESSURE COOKING	MAKES
20 MIN	15 MIN	10 CUPS (2.5 L), APPROX.

PRESSURIZATION	DEPRESSURIZATION	FREEZES
30 MIN	15 MIN	YES

HIGH COOKING TEMPERATURE =
AMPED UP FLAVORS

SHRIMP AND CORN CHOWDER

2	thick slices bacon, diced
1	onion, finely chopped
2 tbsp	butter
3 tbsp	unbleached all-purpose flour
3 cups	(480 g) diced red potatoes, unpeeled
2 cups	(300 g) frozen corn kernels, thawed
4 cups	(1 L) seafood broth (recipe p. 10)
¾ lb	(340 g) fresh or thawed frozen Nordic shrimp
½ cup	(125 ml) 15% or 35% cream
¼ cup	(10 g) finely chopped flat-leaf parsley

Preheat the container of your pressure cooker on the Sauté function for 2 minutes. Brown the bacon and onion in the butter.

Add the flour and cook, stirring, for 1 minute. Add the potatoes, corn and broth. Season with salt and pepper and mix well. Secure the lid and select the Soup function (or set to High pressure). Set the cooking time to 5 minutes.

When ready, depressurize your pressure cooker manually, then remove the lid. Add the shrimp, cream and parsley. Simmer for 1 minute (see note). Adjust the seasoning. Serve the chowder in bowls.

NOTE *Once depressurized, the pressure cooker stays on automatically in stovetop mode. The chowder will be very hot, so there's no need to select a function when simmering for 1 minute.*

PREPARATION	PRESSURE COOKING	SERVINGS
35 MIN	5 MIN	4
PRESSURIZATION	**DEPRESSURIZATION**	**FREEZES**
15 MIN	MANUAL	–

BEEF PHO-STYLE SOUP

½ lb	(225 g) wide rice noodles
1 lb	(450 g) ribeye steak or filet mignon, thinly sliced (see note)
2 cups	(150 g) bean sprouts
1	onion, thinly sliced
2	green onions, thinly sliced
10 cups	(2.5 L) pho beef broth (recipe p. 9), very hot
1 cup	(30 g) cilantro leaves
1 cup	(30 g) Thai basil leaves
1	small bird's eye chili, thinly sliced
1	lime, cut into 8 wedges
	Hoisin sauce, to taste
	Sriracha, to taste

In a large pot of boiling water, cook the noodles for 2 minutes. Drain and divide among four bowls.

Divide the beef slices, bean sprouts, onion and green onions between the bowls. Add the broth. Season with pepper. Serve immediately, leaving everyone to garnish their soup with the herbs, chili, lime and hoisin and sriracha sauces.

NOTE *To easily cut the meat into thin slices, place it in the freezer 2 hours before cutting.*

PREPARATION	COOKING	SERVINGS
15 MIN	2 MIN	4

FREEZES
–

RESTAURANT-WORTHY!

ONE OF OUR
TEAM'S FAVORITES!

GAMJATANG-INSPIRED PORK SOUP WITH CABBAGE AND POTATO

6	green onions, thinly sliced, white and green parts separated
1 tbsp	(15 ml) vegetable oil
6 cups	(1.5 L) soy garlic broth (recipe p. 7)
6	napa cabbage leaves, cut into 6 pieces each
4	potatoes, peeled and cut into 8 pieces each
3 tbsp	(45 ml) fermented chili paste (gochujang)
3 tbsp	(45 ml) fermented soybean paste (doenjang) or miso
1 tbsp	(15 ml) fish sauce
	Cooked ribs from the pork broth (recipe p. 7)
4 cups	(300 g) bean sprouts

Preheat the container of your pressure cooker on the Sauté function for 2 minutes. Soften the white parts of the green onions in the oil.

Add the broth, cabbage, potatoes, chili paste, soybean paste and fish sauce. Season with salt and pepper. Secure the lid and select the Soup function (or set to High pressure). Set the cooking time to 7 minutes.

When ready, depressurize your pressure cooker manually, then remove the lid. Adjust the seasoning. Select the Sauté function. Add the ribs and bean sprouts. Simmer for 2 to 3 minutes, until the meat is warmed through. Garnish with the green parts of the green onions. Serve the soup in large bowls.

PREPARATION	PRESSURE COOKING	SERVINGS
30 MIN	7 MIN	4
PRESSURIZATION	**DEPRESSURIZATION**	**FREEZES**
15 MIN	MANUAL	-

CHICKEN NOODLE SOUP WITH CARROT JUICE

2	carrots, diced
2	stalks celery, diced
1	garlic clove, chopped
½ tsp	turmeric
1 tbsp	(15 ml) olive oil
4 cups	(1 L) chicken broth (recipe p. 8), plus more as needed
2 cups	(500 ml) carrot juice
1 cup	(100 g) crushed spaghettini or angel hair pasta
	Cooked and shredded chicken leg meat from chicken broth (recipe p. 8)
2 tbsp	finely chopped flat-leaf parsley

Preheat the container of your pressure cooker on the Sauté function for 2 minutes. Soften the carrots, celery and garlic with the turmeric in the oil for 2 minutes.

Add the broth and carrot juice. Season with salt and pepper. Secure the lid and select the Soup function (or set to High pressure). Set the cooking time to 5 minutes.

When ready, depressurize your pressure cooker manually, then remove the lid.

Select the Sauté function. Add the spaghettini and simmer for 5 minutes, stirring a few times.

Add the chicken and parsley. Add broth, if needed, to achieve the desired consistency. Adjust the seasoning. Serve the soup in bowls.

PREPARATION	PRESSURE COOKING	SERVINGS
20 MIN	5 MIN	4

PRESSURIZATION	DEPRESSURIZATION	FREEZES
10 MIN	MANUAL	YES

PEA SOUP

2 oz	(55 g) salt pork without the rind, diced
1 tbsp	(15 ml) olive oil
2	carrots, diced
2	stalks celery, diced
1	large onion, finely chopped
1½ cups	(330 g) split yellow peas, rinsed and drained
5 cups	(1.25 L) chicken broth (recipe p. 8), plus more as needed (see note)
1	bay leaf
5 oz	(140 g) cooked ham, diced or torn into pieces (optional) (see note)

Preheat the container of your pressure cooker on the Sauté function for 2 minutes. Brown the salt pork in the oil. Add the carrots, celery and onion. Cook for 5 minutes, stirring a few times. Add the split yellow peas, broth and bay leaf. Season with pepper. Secure the lid and select the Bean function (or set to High pressure). Set the cooking time to 20 minutes.

When ready, depressurize your pressure cooker manually, then remove the lid. Remove and compost the bay leaf. Add the ham, if using. Adjust the seasoning. Add broth, if needed, to achieve the desired consistency. Serve the soup in bowls. Accompany with slices of country bread, if desired.

NOTE *If you made the maple and beer ham (recipe p. 111), you can use 2 cups (500 ml) of the cooking juice and 3 cups (750 ml) of water. Use the cooked ham to add to the soup.*

PREPARATION	PRESSURE COOKING	SERVINGS
25 MIN	20 MIN	6

PRESSURIZATION	DEPRESSURIZATION	FREEZES
10 MIN	MANUAL	YES

CREAM OF CARROT SOUP

1	small onion, chopped
2 tbsp	butter
5 cups	(1.25 L) chicken broth (recipe p. 8)
3 cups	(390 g) carrots, sliced into rounds (about 7 carrots)
1	potato, peeled and cubed

Preheat the container of your pressure cooker on the Sauté function for 2 minutes. Soften the onion in the butter for 2 minutes.

Add the remaining ingredients. Season with salt and pepper. Secure the lid and select the Soup function (or set to High pressure). Set the cooking time to 7 minutes.

When ready, depressurize your pressure cooker manually, then remove the lid.

In a blender, purée the soup until smooth. Adjust the seasoning. Divide the soup among six bowls.

PREPARATION	PRESSURE COOKING	SERVINGS
25 MIN	7 MIN	6
PRESSURIZATION	**DEPRESSURIZATION**	**FREEZES**
10 MIN	MANUAL	YES

TOM KHA-STYLE CHICKEN AND COCONUT MILK SOUP

4	green onions, thinly sliced, white and green parts separated	4 oz	(115 g) shiitake mushrooms, stems removed, thinly sliced
1	piece fresh ginger or galangal 3 inches (7.5 cm) long, washed and cut into 4 slices (see note)	2 tbsp	(30 ml) fish sauce
		1–2 tbsp	(15 to 30 ml) Thai chili paste or 2 lightly crushed bird's eye chilies
1	stalk lemongrass, crushed	1 can	(14 oz/398 ml) coconut milk
1 tbsp	(15 ml) vegetable oil	3 tbsp	(45 ml) lime juice
6	kaffir lime leaves or 2 tbsp (30 ml) lime juice (see note)	2 tsp	cane or brown sugar
		1	lime, cut into wedges
		¼ cup	(10 g) cilantro leaves
4 cups	(1 L) chicken broth (recipe p. 8)		
1 lb	(450 g) boneless, skinless chicken thighs, diced or thinly sliced		

Preheat the container of your pressure cooker on the Sauté function for 2 minutes. Soften the white parts of the green onions, ginger and lemongrass in the oil for 2 minutes.

Add the lime leaves, broth, chicken, mushrooms, fish sauce and chili paste. Secure the lid and select the Soup function (or set to High pressure). Set the cooking time to 7 minutes.

When ready, let your pressure cooker depressurize naturally (about 10 minutes), then remove the lid. Remove the ginger, lemongrass and lime leaves and compost. Stir in the coconut milk, lime juice and cane sugar. Adjust the seasoning.

Divide the soup among four large bowls, filled with cooked rice noodles, if desired. Garnish with the green parts of the green onions, lime wedges and cilantro.

NOTES *What is the difference between a Tom Yum and a Tom Kha soup? Coconut milk is added to the latter.*

Galangal is a rhizome that resembles ginger. You'll find it in most Asian grocery stores.

Also known as bergamot, combava leaves or makrut, kaffir lime leaves can be found dried or fresh in Asian grocery stores and in some supermarkets.

PREPARATION 35 MIN	**PRESSURE COOKING** 7 MIN	**SERVINGS** 4
PRESSURIZATION 10 MIN	**DEPRESSURIZATION** 10 MIN	**FREEZES** –

LENTIL AND BELL PEPPER SOUP

2	red bell peppers, seeded and diced
1	onion, chopped
1	garlic clove, finely chopped
2 tbsp	(30 ml) olive oil
½ tsp	turmeric
½ tsp	ground cumin
½ tsp	ground coriander
4 cups	(1 L) beef, chicken or vegetable broth (recipes p. 9, p. 8 and p. 6)
1 cup	(190 g) red lentils, rinsed and drained
2 tbsp	(30 ml) tomato paste
1 tbsp	(15 ml) apple cider vinegar
2 tbsp	finely chopped cilantro
2	green onions, chopped

Preheat the container of your pressure cooker on the Sauté function for 2 minutes. Soften the peppers, onion and garlic in the oil for 2 minutes. Add the spices and cook, stirring, for 1 minute.

Add the broth, lentils, tomato paste and vinegar. Season with salt and pepper and mix well. Secure the lid and select the Soup function (or set to High pressure). Set the cooking time to 10 minutes.

When ready, depressurize your pressure cooker manually, then remove the lid. Adjust the seasoning. Add the cilantro and green onions. Divide the soup among four bowls. Serve with toasted bread, if desired.

PREPARATION	PRESSURE COOKING	SERVINGS
20 MIN	10 MIN	4

PRESSURIZATION	DEPRESSURIZATION	FREEZES
10 MIN	MANUAL	YES

MINESTRONE WITH WINTER VEGETABLES

1 cup	(200 g) dried large white beans
1	onion, chopped
1	leek, white part only, diced
2 tbsp	(30 ml) olive oil
¾ cup	(180 ml) white wine
5 cups	(1.25 L) vegetable broth (recipe p. 6)
3 cups	(450 g) cubed butternut squash
3 cups	(255 g) cubed Savoy cabbage
2	carrots, sliced into rounds

Place the beans in a large bowl. Cover with water and soak for 8 hours or overnight at room temperature. Add water as needed so that the beans are always well covered. Rinse and drain.

Preheat the container of your pressure cooker on the Sauté function for 2 minutes. Soften the onion and leek in the oil. Deglaze with the wine and let reduce for 2 minutes.

Add the broth and beans. Secure the lid and select the Bean function (or set to High pressure). Set the cooking time to 24 minutes.

When ready, depressurize your pressure cooker manually, then remove the lid. Add the remaining ingredients. Season with salt and pepper and mix well. Secure the lid and select the Soup function (or set to High pressure). Set the cooking time to 4 minutes.

When ready, depressurize your pressure cooker manually, then remove the lid. Adjust the seasoning. Serve the soup in bowls. Serve with slices of country bread, if desired.

PREPARATION	PRESSURIZATION	SERVINGS
30 MIN	10 MIN	4 TO 6
SOAKING	**PRESSURE COOKING**	**FREEZES**
8 H	28 MIN	–
	DEPRESSURIZATION	
	MANUAL	

baby potatoes and asparagus with
Parmesan butter (page 45)

TWO DIFFERENT
COOKING TIMES,
ONE DELICIOUS DISH!

VEGETABLES

Beyond potatoes—an ingredient whose cooking time is noticeably accelerated in the pressure cooker—many other vegetables also work well in this appliance. In addition to maintaining their flavors and nutrients, vegetables cook evenly, all thanks to the steam under pressure. So whether it's to replenish those vegetable reserves in the freezer or to prepare a healthy meal by barely lifting a finger, this is a great way to cook vegetables fast.

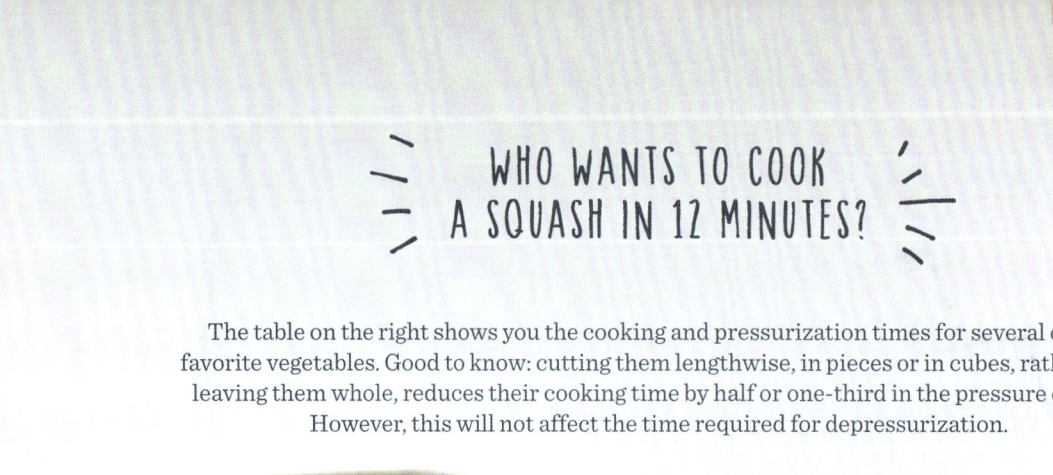

WHO WANTS TO COOK
A SQUASH IN 12 MINUTES?

The table on the right shows you the cooking and pressurization times for several of our favorite vegetables. Good to know: cutting them lengthwise, in pieces or in cubes, rather than leaving them whole, reduces their cooking time by half or one-third in the pressure cooker. However, this will not affect the time required for depressurization.

**acorn squash with
sage butter (page 44)**

COOKING VEGETABLES

To cook any of the vegetables in the list below, pour 1 cup (250 ml) of cold water into the container of your pressure cooker. Place the silicone grill at the bottom of the container, unless otherwise indicated, then add the vegetable of your choice.

VEGETABLE	Function	Cooking Time	Pressurization Time
Asparagus, large, trimmed	Low	1 minute	5 to 6 minutes
Beans, yellow or green, whole	High	1 minute	5 to 7 minutes
Beets, whole	High	15 to 25 minutes	7 to 10 minutes
Beets, peeled and cubed	High	6 minutes	8 to 10 minutes
Broccoli, cut into large florets	Low	2 minutes	5 to 6 minutes
Brussels sprouts, whole	High	4 minutes	5 to 6 minutes
Carrots, halved lengthwise	High	6 minutes	5 to 7 minutes
Carrots, cut into 2-inch (5 cm) pieces	High	8 minutes	5 to 7 minutes
Cauliflower, cut into large florets	Low	3 minutes	5 to 8 minutes
Corncobs, whole (without the silicone grill)	High	3 minutes	4 to 5 minutes
Potatoes, cubed	High	5 minutes	8 to 10 minutes
Potatoes, whole (peeled or not)	High	12 to 20 minutes	5 to 8 minutes
Potatoes, baby, whole	High	6 to 10 minutes	6 to 9 minutes
Rutabaga, cubed	High	6 minutes	5 to 8 minutes
Squash, acorn, halved, seeds removed (see note)	High	12 minutes	4 to 6 minutes
Squash, butternut, cubed, seeds removed (see note)	High	4 minutes	5 to 6 minutes
Squash, spaghetti, cut into 2 pieces, seeds removed	High	12 minutes	7 to 9 minutes
Sweet potatoes, cubed	High	4 minutes	5 to 8 minutes

Place the squash cut-side down.

Cooking times may vary depending on the size of the vegetable. The minimum cooking times listed above are for a diameter or thickness of 1 ½ inches (4 cm).

CONFIT GARLIC

3	heads garlic
1 tbsp	(15 ml) olive oil

On a work surface, cut off the tops of the garlic heads to expose the cloves. Brush with the oil. Season with salt.

Pour 1 cup (250 ml) of water into the container of the pressure cooker. Place the silicone grill in it. Add the garlic heads, cut-side up. Secure the lid and set to High pressure. Set the cooking time to 16 minutes.

When ready, let your pressure cooker depressurize naturally (about 10 minutes), then remove the lid. Remove the garlic heads from the container with tongs, then let cool on a plate. Squeeze the garlic heads to extract the flesh (see note). The confit garlic will keep for up to 2 weeks in an airtight container in the refrigerator.

A delicious spread for toast to serve with soup.

NOTE *The recipe multiplies easily. You can freeze whole heads or the extracted flesh.*

PREPARATION	PRESSURE COOKING	MAKES
5 MIN	16 MIN	3 HEADS

PRESSURIZATION	DEPRESSURIZATION	FREEZES
5 MIN	10 MIN	YES

GARLIC MASHED POTATOES

2.2 lb	**(1 kg) russet or Yukon Gold potatoes, washed and halved**
4	**garlic cloves, peeled**
¼ cup	**(55 g) butter, softened**
½ cup	**(125 ml) milk, warm**

Pour 1 cup (250 ml) of water into the container of the pressure cooker. Place the silicone grill in it. Add the potatoes and garlic. Secure the lid and select the Root vegetable function (or set to High pressure). Set the cooking time to 15 minutes.

When ready, depressurize your pressure cooker manually, then remove the lid. Using a potato ricer, crush a piece of potato at a time, cut-side down, with garlic. Remove the peel from the ricer between each piece and compost. Add the butter and milk. Season with salt and pepper and mix well.

PREPARATION	PRESSURE COOKING	SERVINGS
20 MIN	15 MIN	6

PRESSURIZATION	DEPRESSURIZATION	FREEZES
10 MIN	MANUAL	–

YOU DON'T EVEN NEED
TO PEEL THE POTATOES!

BEET, QUINOA AND WATERMELON SALAD

6	medium beets
3 tbsp	(45 ml) red wine vinegar
1 cup	(180 g) quinoa, cooked and cooled (table p. 69)
3 cups	(450 g) diced, seeded watermelon
4 cups	(100 g) arugula, coarsely chopped
3 tbsp	(45 ml) olive oil
½ lb	(225 g) fresh unripened goat cheese, crumbled (optional)

Pour 1 cup (250 ml) of water into the container of the pressure cooker. Place the silicone grill in it, then add the beets. Secure the lid and select the Root vegetable function (or set to High pressure). Set the cooking time to 20 minutes.

When ready, depressurize your pressure cooker manually, then remove the lid. Cool the beets under running cold water. Peel the beets and dice them.

In a large bowl, combine the beets and vinegar. Add the quinoa, watermelon, arugula and oil. Season with salt and pepper and mix well. Place the salad on a serving plate. Top with goat cheese, if using.

PREPARATION	PRESSURE COOKING	SERVINGS
20 MIN	20 MIN	6

PRESSURIZATION	DEPRESSURIZATION	FREEZES
10 MIN	MANUAL	–

BRAISED CABBAGE WITH SAUSAGES AND SWEET POTATOES

1 lb	(450 g) mild or spicy Italian sausages, cut into 2 pieces (4 to 5 sausages)
1 tbsp	(15 ml) olive oil
6 cups	(510 g) green cabbage, cut into 1-inch (2.5 cm) wide strips
3	garlic cloves, chopped
4 cups	(600 g) peeled sweet potatoes, cut into large cubes
½ cup	(125 ml) chicken broth (recipe p. 8)
½ tsp	ground black pepper
¼ tsp	caraway seeds

Preheat the container of your pressure cooker on the Sauté function for 2 minutes. Brown the sausages on each side in the oil. Set aside on a plate.

Soften the cabbage in the oil for 2 minutes. Season with salt. Add the remaining ingredients and the sausages. Mix well. Secure the lid and select the Root vegetable function (or set to High pressure). Set the cooking time to 8 minutes.

When ready, depressurize your pressure cooker manually, then remove the lid. Adjust the seasoning.

PREPARATION	PRESSURE COOKING	SERVINGS
25 MIN	8 MIN	4
PRESSURIZATION	**DEPRESSURIZATION**	**FREEZES**
5 MIN	MANUAL	–

CORN ON THE COB
WITH PESTO BUTTER

8	corncobs, husks removed
¼ cup	(55 g) unsalted butter, softened
¼ cup	(20 g) grated fresh Parmesan cheese
¼ cup	(60 ml) homemade or store-bought pesto

Stand the corncobs vertically in the container of your pressure cooker (see note). Add 1 cup (250 ml) of water. Secure the lid and set to High pressure. Set the cooking time to 3 minutes.

When ready, depressurize your pressure cooker manually, then remove the lid.

Meanwhile, in a bowl, combine the butter with the cheese and pesto. Season with pepper.

Garnish the hot corn with the pesto butter.

NOTE *Depending on the size of the corncobs, you can cut them or place them differently in the container.*

PREPARATION	PRESSURE COOKING	SERVINGS
10 MIN	3 MIN	4

PRESSURIZATION	DEPRESSURIZATION	FREEZES
10 MIN	MANUAL	–

SPAGHETTI SQUASH WITH TOMATOES, ONIONS AND OLIVES

1	spaghetti squash (about 3 lb/1.4 kg)
¼ cup	(60 ml) olive oil
2	onions, thinly sliced
1	garlic clove, finely chopped
½ cup	(125 ml) chicken broth (recipe p. 8)
2 cups	(280 g) cherry tomatoes
¼ cup	(35 g) green and black olives, pitted and thinly sliced
¾ cup	(100 g) diced feta cheese
¼ cup	(10 g) thinly sliced basil leaves

On a work surface, cut the squash in half. Using a spoon, remove the seeds and compost. Season the squash with salt and pepper.

Pour 1 cup (250 ml) of water into the container of the pressure cooker. Place the silicone grill in it, then add the squash, cut-side down. Secure the lid and select the Root vegetable function (or set to High pressure). Set the cooking time to 12 minutes.

When ready, depressurize your pressure cooker manually, then remove the lid. Let the squash cool.

Shred the flesh with a fork. Place the flesh in a bowl and compost the skin. Add 2 tbsp (30 ml) of oil. Season with salt and pepper and mix well. Set aside, cover and keep warm.

Meanwhile, in a skillet over medium-high heat, brown the onions in the remaining 2 tbsp (30 ml) of oil. Season with salt and pepper. Add the garlic and cook for 1 minute, stirring. Add the broth, tomatoes and olives. Cover and simmer for 5 minutes or until the tomatoes begin to burst. Remove from the heat. Stir in the cheese. Adjust the seasoning.

Divide the spaghetti squash among four plates, forming a nest. Top with the onion mixture and sprinkle with the basil.

NOTE *You can serve spaghetti squash as a side vegetable. After cooking the squash under pressure, simply brown the flesh in 2 tbsp butter in a non-stick skillet.*

PREPARATION 35 MIN	12 MIN	**FREEZES** –
	DEPRESSURIZATION	
PRESSURIZATION 5 MIN	MANUAL	
	SERVINGS	
PRESSURE COOKING	4	

ACORN SQUASH
WITH SAGE BUTTER

2	small acorn squash, halved, seeds removed
¼ cup	(55 g) butter
4	sage leaves

Pour 1 cup (250 ml) of water into the container of your pressure cooker. Place the silicone grill in it, then place the squash cut-side down. Secure the lid and select the Root vegetable function (or set to High pressure). Set the cooking time to 12 minutes.

When ready, depressurize your pressure cooker manually, then remove the lid. Remove the squash from the container. Using a knife, score the flesh in a criss-cross pattern. Season with salt and pepper.

In a large non-stick skillet over medium heat, warm the butter with the sage leaves. Place the squash halves cut-side down in the butter. Cook until nicely browned. Transfer the squash to a serving plate, then drizzle with the butter. Delicious served with grilled meat.

PREPARATION	PRESSURE COOKING	SERVINGS
15 MIN	12 MIN	4

PRESSURIZATION	DEPRESSURIZATION	FREEZES
5 MIN	MANUAL	–

BABY POTATOES AND ASPARAGUS WITH PARMESAN BUTTER

¼ cup	(55 g) salted butter, melted
¼ cup	(20 g) finely grated fresh Parmesan cheese
¼ cup	(10 g) mixed finely chopped herbs (dill, chives and parsley), plus more for serving
1	small garlic clove, finely chopped
1 lb	(450 g) baby potatoes, halved
¾ lb	(340 g) large asparagus, trimmed (see note)

In a large bowl, combine the butter, cheese, herbs and garlic. Season with pepper. Set aside.

Pour 1 cup (250 ml) of water into the container of the pressure cooker. Place the silicone grill in it, then add the potatoes. Secure the lid and select the Root vegetable function (or set to High pressure). Set the cooking time to 5 minutes.

When ready, depressurize your pressure cooker manually, then remove the lid. Add the asparagus. Secure the lid and select the Root vegetable function (or set to High pressure). Set the cooking time to 1 minute.

When ready, depressurize your pressure cooker manually, then remove the lid. Drain the vegetables and add them to the bowl of butter. Toss well to coat thoroughly. Adjust the seasoning. Transfer the vegetables to a serving plate. Sprinkle with more herbs. Delicious served with steak or grilled chicken.

NOTE *Use large asparagus for this recipe. Small asparagus tends to overcook.*

PREPARATION	PRESSURE COOKING	SERVINGS
15 MIN	6 MIN	4

PRESSURIZATION	DEPRESSURIZATION	FREEZES
10 MIN	MANUAL	–

pulled bbq beef
with beer (page 60)

SERVED WITH SQUASH AND
ROOT VEGETABLES, THIS PULLED
MEAT IS THE ULTIMATE
IN COMFORT FOOD.

MEAT

Cooking meat in a pressure cooker is the best. It's so easy and effective that you can even make several dishes in a row, to freeze. While these types of recipes usually require a long cooking time in the oven—often impossible to do during the week—the ones in this chapter will make mealtimes from Monday to Friday a breeze. Note that, with the exception of chicken, all meat is cut into slices rather than pieces before being added to the pressure cooker. This ensures the cooking is more even. The result is such tender meat, it's incomparable to that cooked in the slow cooker (even if we love that just as much!).

SWEET AND SALTY PULLED PORK

4 lb	(1.8 kg) boneless pork shoulder roast without the rind, cut into 6 slices
2 tbsp	(30 ml) vegetable oil
¾ cup	(160 g) brown sugar
⅓ cup	(75 ml) soy sauce
¼ cup	(60 ml) water
¼ cup	(60 ml) mild Thai green curry paste
6	green onions, finely chopped, white and green parts separated
½ cup	(75 g) roasted cashews or peanuts, chopped

Preheat the container of your pressure cooker on the Sauté function for 2 minutes. Brown the meat in the oil. Season with salt and pepper.

Add the brown sugar, soy sauce, water, curry paste and the white parts of the green onions. Season with salt and pepper and mix well. Secure the lid and select the Meat function (or set to High pressure). Set the cooking time to 45 minutes.

When ready, let your pressure cooker depressurize naturally (about 15 minutes), then remove the lid. Remove the meat from the container. Using a fork, break up the meat into large pieces, taking care to remove the fat. Place the meat in a bowl. Add the cooking juice to taste. Adjust the seasoning.

Garnish with the cashews and the green parts of the green onions. Serve the pulled pork with rice and vegetables, if desired.

PREPARATION	PRESSURE COOKING	SERVINGS
20 MIN	45 MIN	6
PRESSURIZATION	**DEPRESSURIZATION**	**FREEZES**
5 MIN	15 MIN	YES

MEDITERRANEAN-INSPIRED CHICKEN

2 tbsp	(30 ml) olive oil
1 tbsp	(15 ml) tomato paste
1 tsp	sweet paprika
1 tsp	dried oregano
1 tsp	red pepper flakes
½ tsp	onion powder
½ tsp	ground allspice
½ tsp	salt
4	garlic cloves, finely chopped
2 lb	(900 g) boneless, skinless chicken thighs
1	lemon, washed and halved

In a bowl, combine the oil, tomato paste, spices, salt and garlic. Add the chicken and toss to coat thoroughly.

Pour 1 cup (250 ml) of water into the container of the pressure cooker. Place the silicone grill in it, then add the chicken mixture and lemon halves. Secure the lid and select the Poultry function (or set to High pressure). Set the cooking time to 8 minutes.

When ready, let your pressure cooker depressurize naturally (about 10 minutes), then remove the lid. Squeeze the juice of the lemon halves over the chicken. Serve with brown rice (table p. 69), hummus (recipe p. 86) and a green salad, if desired.

PREPARATION	PRESSURE COOKING	SERVINGS
15 MIN	8 MIN	6
PRESSURIZATION	**DEPRESSURIZATION**	**FREEZES**
10 MIN	10 MIN	–

MIXED WITH SPICES AND LEMON, THIS CHICKEN COMES OUT FULL OF FLAVOR IN JUST 10 MINUTES.

BEEF WITH CHERRY TOMATOES

2.2 lb	(1 kg) boneless beef blade roast, cut into 6 slices
2 tbsp	(30 ml) olive oil
2	onions, cut into thin wedges
2	garlic cloves, chopped
½ cup	(125 ml) beef broth (recipe p. 9)
2 tbsp	(30 ml) whole-grain mustard
½ tsp	dried oregano
2 cups	(280 g) cherry tomatoes
2 tbsp	finely chopped flat-leaf parsley

Preheat the container of your pressure cooker on the Sauté function for 2 minutes. Brown the beef in the oil. Season with salt and pepper. Set the meat aside on a plate.

Add the onions and garlic. Brown them well. Add the meat, broth, mustard and oregano. Season with salt and pepper and mix well. Secure the lid and select the Meat function (or set to High pressure). Set the cooking time to 45 minutes.

When ready, let your pressure cooker depressurize naturally (about 15 minutes), then remove the lid. Select the Sauté function. Break up the meat into large pieces. Add the tomatoes and simmer until tender, about 7 minutes. Sprinkle with the parsley. Delicious with egg noodles.

PREPARATION	PRESSURE COOKING	SERVINGS
30 MIN	45 MIN	4 TO 6

PRESSURIZATION	DEPRESSURIZATION	FREEZES
5 MIN	15 MIN	–

OUR NEW
FAVORITE PRESSURE
COOKER RECIPE.
FOR REAL.

PULLED CHICKEN CARNITAS TACOS

CHICKEN

½ cup	(125 ml) orange juice
¼ cup	(60 ml) lime juice
1 tbsp	chili powder
2 tsp	ground cumin
1 tsp	dried oregano
4	garlic cloves, finely chopped
4	green onions, finely chopped
2 lb	(900 g) boneless, skinless chicken thighs (see note)

TORTILLAS AND GARNISHES

8	soft wheat tortillas about 7 inches (18 cm) in diameter
	Grated mozzarella cheese, to taste
	Homemade or store-bought salsa, to taste
	Sour cream, to taste
1	ripe avocado, sliced
1	tomato, diced
1	onion, thinly sliced
	Cilantro leaves, to taste

CHICKEN

In the container of your pressure cooker, combine all the ingredients except for the chicken.

Add the chicken and toss to coat thoroughly. Season with salt and pepper. Secure the lid and select the Poultry function (or set to High pressure). Set the cooking time to 10 minutes.

When ready, let your pressure cooker depressurize naturally (about 10 minutes), then remove the lid. Remove the chicken from the pressure cooker and shred it. Set the cooking juice aside.

With the rack in the highest position, preheat the oven to broil. Line a baking sheet with foil.

Spread the pulled chicken out on the prepared baking sheet. Drizzle with some of the cooking juice. Broil for 5 minutes or until nicely browned, turning the chicken over once. Remove from the oven and add more cooking juice, to taste. Transfer to a serving plate.

TORTILLAS AND GARNISHES

Place the chicken, tortillas and garnishes in the center of the table. Let each person garnish their own tortillas.

NOTE *The recipe is also delicious with cubed pork shoulder. The pressure-cooking time would be 20 minutes on the Meat function (or set to High pressure).*

PREPARATION	PRESSURE COOKING	SERVINGS
30 MIN	10 MIN	4 TO 6

PRESSURIZATION	DEPRESSURIZATION	FREEZES
10 MIN	10 MIN	YES (MEAT ONLY)

PULLED PORK GNOCCHI

2	large onions, thinly sliced
¼ cup	(55 g) butter
2	garlic cloves, chopped
2 lb	(900 g) boneless pork shoulder without the rind, cut into 6 slices
1 cup	(250 ml) pork or chicken broth (recipes p. 7 and p. 8)
1 tbsp	(15 ml) apple cider vinegar
2	packages (12 oz/350 g) fresh or vacuum-sealed gnocchi
2 tbsp	(30 ml) olive oil
¼ cup	(10 g) finely chopped flat-leaf parsley (see note)

Preheat the container of your pressure cooker on the Sauté function for 2 minutes. Brown the onions in half of the butter. Add the garlic.

Meanwhile, in a large skillet over high heat, brown the pork in the remaining butter. Season with salt and pepper. Transfer to the pressure cooker. Add the broth and vinegar. Secure the lid and select the Meat function (or set to High pressure). Set the cooking time to 45 minutes.

When ready, let your pressure cooker depressurize naturally (about 15 minutes), then remove the lid. Remove the meat from the pressure cooker and shred it, taking care to remove the fat. Set the cooking juice aside.

Meanwhile, with the rack in the middle position, preheat the oven to 425°F (220°C).

On a non-stick baking sheet, toss the gnocchi with the oil to coat. Bake for 20 minutes, stirring halfway through cooking, or until the gnocchi is golden and crispy.

In a large bowl, combine the gnocchi, parsley, meat and 1 ½ cups (375 ml) of cooking juice. Add more cooking juice.

NOTE *You can replace the parsley with 1 cup (150 g) thawed frozen peas to add freshness to the dish.*

PREPARATION	PRESSURE COOKING	SERVINGS
35 MIN	45 MIN	6
PRESSURIZATION	**DEPRESSURIZATION**	**FREEZES**
5 MIN	15 MIN	YES (MEAT ONLY)

RIBS WITH BBQ SAUCE

RIBS

2 tbsp	brown sugar
1 tbsp	chili powder
2 tsp	salt
1 tsp	ground pepper
1 tsp	dry mustard
½ tsp	onion powder
5 lb	(2.3 kg) baby back pork ribs

BBQ SAUCE

1 tbsp	chili powder
1 tsp	onion powder
½ tsp	garlic powder
2 tbsp	butter
¾ cup	(180 ml) ketchup
¾ cup	(180 ml) apple jelly
¼ cup	(60 ml) apple cider vinegar
2 tbsp	(30 ml) molasses
1 tbsp	(15 ml) Dijon mustard
1 tbsp	(15 ml) Worcestershire sauce
	A few drops Tabasco-style sauce

RIBS

In a bowl, combine the brown sugar and spices.

On a work surface, cut the ribs into sections with 3 or 4 bones each, then sprinkle with the brown sugar mixture, rubbing the meat well on each side.

Pour 1 cup (250 ml) of water into the container of the pressure cooker. Place the silicone grill in it. Place the rib sections standing on the grill. Secure the lid and select the Meat function (or set to High pressure). Set the cooking time to 25 minutes.

When ready, let your pressure cooker depressurize naturally (about 15 minutes), then remove the lid. Remove the ribs from the container. Discard the cooking juice.

BBQ SAUCE

Meanwhile, in a small pot, sauté the spices in the butter for 1 minute, stirring constantly. Add the remaining ingredients. Bring to a boil and simmer for 10 minutes or until the sauce is syrupy. Season with salt and pepper.

Preheat the barbecue grill to medium. Oil the grate.

Grill the ribs for 15 minutes, turning them over frequently and brushing with the barbecue sauce. Serve the ribs with the remaining sauce.

NOTE *Rather than barbecuing the ribs, you can finish cooking them under the broiler. Line a baking sheet with foil. Place the ribs on the prepared baking sheet and brush with the barbecue sauce. Broil the ribs for 5 to 6 minutes on each side, or until caramelized.*

PREPARATION 20 MIN	25 MIN	**FREEZES** -
	DEPRESSURIZATION	
PRESSURIZATION 15 MIN	15 MIN	
	SERVINGS	
PRESSURE COOKING	4 TO 6	

PULLED BBQ BEEF WITH BEER

1	onion, cut into pieces
1	jalapeño pepper, seeded and cut into pieces
2	garlic cloves, halved
½ cup	(125 ml) pale ale
½ cup	(125 ml) ketchup
2 tbsp	(30 ml) white vinegar
2 tbsp	(30 ml) prepared yellow mustard
1 tbsp	brown sugar
1 tbsp	chili powder
1 tbsp	(15 ml) Worcestershire sauce
2.2 lb	(1 kg) boneless beef blade roast, cut into 6 slices

In a blender, purée all the ingredients except the meat until smooth. Pour the sauce into the container of the pressure cooker.

Add the meat and toss to coat thoroughly. Season with salt and pepper. Secure the lid and select the Meat function (or set to High pressure). Set the cooking time to 45 minutes.

When ready, let your pressure cooker depressurize naturally (about 15 minutes), then remove the lid. Remove the meat from the container. Using a fork, shred the meat, taking care to remove the fat. Place the meat in a bowl.

Meanwhile, select the Sauté function and reduce the cooking juice for about 10 minutes, to get a syrupy sauce (see note).

Add the sauce to the meat and toss to coat thoroughly. Adjust the seasoning. Serve pulled beef with cornbread or polenta, in hamburger buns or over sweet potatoes, if desired.

NOTE *You can also serve the meat with a little cooking juice, without reducing it.*

PREPARATION	PRESSURE COOKING	SERVINGS
25 MIN	45 MIN	6
PRESSURIZATION	**DEPRESSURIZATION**	**FREEZES**
10 MIN	15 MIN	YES

PULLED CHICKEN

2 lb (900 g) boneless, skinless chicken thighs
1 cup (250 ml) chicken broth (recipe p. 8)

In the container of your pressure cooker, combine the chicken and broth. Season with salt. Secure the lid and select the Poultry function (or set to High pressure). Set the cooking time to 10 minutes.

When ready, let your pressure cooker depressurize naturally (about 10 minutes), then remove the lid.

Drain the chicken and shred the meat. Place the meat in a bowl. Add the cooking broth, to taste. Set the rest of the broth aside for another use.

PREPARATION	PRESSURE COOKING	MAKES
5 MIN	10 MIN	4 CUPS (680 G), APPROX.

PRESSURIZATION	DEPRESSURIZATION	FREEZES
10 MIN	10 MIN	YES

BUFFALO CHICKEN SALAD

DRESSING

2 oz	(55 g) blue cheese, crumbled
½ cup	(125 ml) mayonnaise
¼ cup	(60 ml) sour cream
2 tbsp	finely chopped parsley
1 tbsp	(15 ml) lemon juice
2 tsp	(10 ml) honey
1	small garlic clove, chopped, or ½ tsp garlic purée (see note)
	Hot sauce, to taste (see note)

SALAD

1	recipe pulled chicken, cooked (recipe p. 61)
1	small iceberg lettuce, cut into thin wedges
2	stalks celery, thinly sliced
½ cup	(75 g) frozen corn kernels, thawed
¼ cup	(10 g) finely chopped parsley

DRESSING

In a bowl, whisk all the ingredients together. Season with salt and pepper.

ASSEMBLY

Divide the chicken and lettuce among four bowls. Add the celery, corn and parsley. Drizzle with the dressing to serve.

NOTES *We love garlic purée in recipes that call for raw garlic because the flavor is sweeter.*

We used the classic Frank's RedHot sauce, which often accompanies Buffalo chicken wings. You can use your favorite vinegar-based hot sauce.

PREPARATION	SERVINGS	FREEZES
15 MIN	4	–

BBQ PULLED PORK

½ cup	(125 ml) ketchup	1 tbsp	(15 ml) Worcestershire sauce	½ tsp	garlic powder
¼ cup	(60 ml) apple cider vinegar			3 lb	(1.4 kg) boneless pork shoulder roast without the rind, cut into 6 slices
¼ cup	(60 ml) apple jelly	1 tsp	onion powder		
2 tbsp	(30 ml) molasses	1 tsp	Tabasco-style sauce		

In the container of your pressure cooker, combine all the ingredients except for the meat.

Add the meat and toss to coat thoroughly. Season with salt and pepper. Secure the lid and select the Meat function (or set to High pressure). Set the cooking time to 45 minutes.

When ready, let your pressure cooker depressurize naturally (about 15 minutes), then remove the lid. Remove the meat from the container. Using a fork, shred the meat, taking care to remove the fat. Place the meat in a bowl.

Meanwhile, select the Sauté function and reduce the cooking juice for about 10 minutes, to obtain a syrupy sauce (see note).

Add the sauce to the meat and toss to coat thoroughly. Adjust the seasoning. Serve the pulled pork with cornbread or polenta, in hamburger buns or over sweet potatoes, if desired.

NOTE *You can also serve the meat with a little cooking juice, without reducing it.*

PREPARATION 25 MIN	**PRESSURE COOKING** 45 MIN	**SERVINGS** 6
PRESSURIZATION 10 MIN	**DEPRESSURIZATION** 15 MIN	**FREEZES** YES

\ l / ,

MEAT THAT'S READY TO ADD TO BREAD, BUNS OR TORTILLAS: SO CONVENIENT!

/ / | \ `

red lentil dahl
(page 73)

LEGUMES & GRAINS

There are so many benefits to eating legumes and grains: they're economical, nutritious, healthy and satisfying. Plus, the pressure cooker cuts their usual cooking time in half. Here we revisit traditional recipes and make them better— and faster—than ever!

COOKING LEGUMES

LEGUME	Amount of Water for 1 Cup of Legumes	Cooking Time with Presoak	Cooking Time without Presoak	Pressurization Time
Brown lentils	2 cups (500 ml)	–	8 minutes	5 minutes
Chickpeas	3 cups (750 ml)	25 minutes	–	10 minutes
Green lentils	2 cups (500 ml)	–	8 minutes	5 minutes
Large red beans	3 cups (750 ml)	22 minutes	50 minutes	7 to 10 minutes
Large white beans	3 cups (750 ml)	22 minutes	50 minutes	7 to 10 minutes
Small black beans	3 cups (750 ml)	18 minutes	45 minutes	7 to 10 minutes
Small red beans	3 cups (750 ml)	18 minutes	50 minutes	7 to 10 minutes
Small white beans	3 cups (750 ml)	15 minutes	30 minutes	7 to 10 minutes

With the pressure cooker, you have the choice of whether or not to soak most legumes beforehand, which is not always the case with traditional cooking methods. In our recipes, we have chosen to soak beans and chickpeas for a faster cooking time. For soaking, place the beans in a bowl. Cover with water and let soak for 12 hours or overnight at room temperature. Add water as needed so that the beans are always well covered. Rinse and drain.

Unsoaked legumes should be rinsed well and drained before cooking.

When cooking legumes, manual depressurization is preferred. You can double the quantities of legumes listed above without modifying the cooking or pressurization time.

Once the legumes are cooked, drain them and rinse under cold water to stop the cooking. Perfect for adding to a soup or salad. They can also be frozen!

COOKING GRAINS

GRAIN	Amount of Water per 1 Cup of Grains	Cooking Time	Pressurization Time
Basmati rice	1 cup (250 ml)	10 minutes	5 minutes
Brown basmati rice	1¼ cups (310 ml)	17 minutes	5 minutes
Hulled barley	2 cups (500 ml)	25 minutes	6 minutes
Long-grain brown rice	1¼ cups (310 ml)	15 minutes	5 minutes
Long-grain white rice	1 cup (250 ml)	10 minutes	5 minutes
Pearl barley	2 cups (500 ml)	20 minutes	6 minutes
Quinoa	2 cups (500 ml)	6 minutes	6 minutes
Soft wheat grains	1½ cups (375 ml)	50 minutes	5 minutes
Sushi rice (Calrose)	1¼ cups (310 ml)	10 minutes	5 minutes
Wild rice	1½ cups (310 ml)	35 minutes	5 minutes

All grains must be rinsed well and drained before cooking. When cooking grains, manual depressurization is preferred. You can double the quantities of grains listed above without modifying the cooking or pressurization time.

For quinoa and all rices, after depressurizing, season and mix well to break up the grains. Cover and let rest for 5 minutes.

YOU HAVE MORE CONTROL OVER THE SALT CONTENT WHEN YOU USE DRIED BEANS AND COOK THEM IN THE PRESSURE COOKER—NO MORE CANNED BEANS!

RED BEANS AND RICE

1 cup	(200 g) dried small red beans
2	thick slices bacon, diced
1	large onion, chopped
3	garlic cloves, finely chopped
2 tbsp	(30 ml) vegetable oil
2	stalks celery, thinly sliced
1 can	(14 oz/398 ml) diced tomatoes
1 cup	(250 ml) chicken or vegetable broth (recipes p. 8 and p. 6)
1 tbsp	(15 ml) Worcestershire sauce
1 tsp	(5 ml) Tabasco-style sauce
4	mild or spicy Italian sausages, blanched and sliced on an angle
	Finely chopped flat-leaf parsley, to taste

Place the beans in a bowl. Cover with water and let soak for 12 hours or overnight at room temperature. Add water as needed so that the beans are always well covered. Rinse and drain.

Preheat the container of your pressure cooker on the Sauté function for 2 minutes. Brown the bacon with the onion and garlic in 1 tbsp (15 ml) of oil. Add the celery, tomatoes, broth, sauces and beans. Season with salt and pepper and mix well. Secure the lid and select the Bean function (or set to High pressure). Set the cooking time to 30 minutes.

When ready, depressurize your pressure cooker manually, then remove the lid. Adjust the seasoning.

Meanwhile, in a non-stick skillet over medium-high heat, brown the sausages in the remaining 1 tbsp (15 ml) of oil.

Serve the beans over white rice or dirty rice (p. 72), if desired. Top with the cooked sausages and parsley.

PREPARATION	PRESSURIZATION	SERVINGS
25 MIN	10 MIN	4
SOAKING	**PRESSURE COOKING**	**FREEZES**
12 H	30 MIN	YES
	DEPRESSURIZATION	
	MANUAL	

cajun-style dirty rice
(page 72)

CAJUN-STYLE DIRTY RICE

¾ lb	(340 g) lean ground pork
1 tbsp	(15 ml) vegetable oil
1	onion, finely chopped
2	garlic cloves, finely chopped
1 tsp	sweet paprika
1 tsp	ground celery seeds
2	stalks celery, diced
1	small green or yellow bell pepper, seeded and diced
1½ cups	(300 g) long-grain white rice, rinsed well and drained
1½ cups	(375 ml) beef or pork broth (recipes p. 9 and p. 7)
1 tbsp	(15 ml) Worcestershire sauce
1 tsp	(5 ml) Tabasco-style sauce
	Finely chopped flat-leaf parsley (optional)

Preheat the container of your pressure cooker on the Sauté function for 2 minutes. Brown the pork in the oil, breaking it up with a wooden spoon. Season with salt and pepper. Add the onion, garlic and spices. Cook, stirring, for 2 minutes.

Add the remaining ingredients except for the parsley. Secure the lid and set to High pressure. Set the cooking time to 10 minutes.

When ready, depressurize your pressure cooker manually, then remove the lid. Mix well to fluff the rice. Cover and let rest for 5 minutes. Adjust the seasoning. Garnish with parsley.

PREPARATION	PRESSURE COOKING	SERVINGS
25 MIN	10 MIN	4
PRESSURIZATION	**DEPRESSURIZATION**	**FREEZES**
5 MIN	MANUAL	–

RED LENTIL DAHL

1	onion, finely chopped
2 tbsp	ghee or butter
3	garlic cloves, finely chopped
1	piece fresh ginger 1 inch (2.5 cm) long, peeled and halved
1 tbsp	turmeric
1 tbsp	garam masala
1 tsp	ground cumin
¼ tsp	red pepper flakes
2½ cups	(625 ml) vegetable or chicken broth (recipes p. 6 and p. 8), plus more as needed
1½ cups	(285 g) dried red lentils, rinsed and drained
	Cooked basmati rice
	Plain yogurt (optional)
	Finely chopped cilantro or flat-leaf parsley (optional)
1	cauliflower, cut into florets, steamed or grilled (optional)
	Lime or lemon wedges (optional)

Preheat the container of your pressure cooker on the Sauté function for 2 minutes. Brown the onion in the ghee. Add the garlic, ginger and spices. Cook, stirring, for 2 minutes.

Add the broth and lentils. Season with salt and pepper and mix well. Secure the lid and select the Soup function (or set to High pressure). Set the cooking time to 5 minutes.

When ready, depressurize your pressure cooker manually, then remove the lid. Remove and compost the ginger. Adjust the seasoning. Add broth, if needed, to achieve the desired consistency.

Serve the dahl with the rice and garnishes. Delicious with lamb tikka masala (recipe p. 103).

PREPARATION	PRESSURE COOKING	SERVINGS
25 MIN	5 MIN	4
PRESSURIZATION	**DEPRESSURIZATION**	**FREEZES**
5 MIN	MANUAL	YES

RICE PILAF

1	onion, finely chopped
2 tbsp	butter
1½ cups	(300 g) long-grain white rice, rinsed well and drained
1	cinnamon stick 2 inches (5 cm) long
1 tsp	turmeric
2 tbsp	dried currants
¼ cup	(30 g) finely sliced almonds, roasted
1½ cups	(375 ml) chicken broth (recipe p. 8)

Preheat the container of your pressure cooker on the Sauté function for 2 minutes. Soften the onion in the butter for 2 minutes. Add the rice and stir to coat.

Add the remaining ingredients. Season with salt and pepper and mix well. Secure the lid and set to High pressure. Set the cooking time to 12 minutes.

When ready, depressurize your pressure cooker manually, then remove the lid. Mix well to fluff the rice. Remove and compost the cinnamon stick. Cover and let rest for 5 minutes. Adjust the seasoning. Delicious with roasted chicken.

PREPARATION	PRESSURE COOKING	SERVINGS
15 MIN	12 MIN	4

PRESSURIZATION	DEPRESSURIZATION	FREEZES
5 MIN	MANUAL	-

CHICKEN BURRITO BOWL

CHICKEN

1½ lb	(675 g) boneless, skinless chicken thighs, cubed
1½ cups	(225 g) frozen corn kernels
1 cup	(250 ml) chicken broth (recipe p. 8)
1 cup	(250 ml) medium or spicy store-bought salsa
2 cups	(500 ml) cooked small black beans (table p. 68) (see note)
1 tbsp	chili powder
1 cup	(200 g) long-grain white rice, rinsed well and drained

GARNISH

4 cups	(240 g) thinly sliced iceberg lettuce
1 cup	(100 g) grated orange cheddar cheese
1	tomato, diced
1	ripe avocado, diced and tossed with a squeeze of lemon juice
¼ cup	(10 g) cilantro leaves

CHICKEN

In the container of your pressure cooker, combine the chicken with the corn, broth, salsa, black beans and chili powder. Season with salt and pepper. Sprinkle the rice onto the chicken mixture, without stirring. Secure the lid and select the Poultry function (or set to High pressure). Set the cooking time to 10 minutes.

When ready, depressurize your pressure cooker manually, then remove the lid. Mix well. Cover and let rest for 5 minutes. Adjust the seasoning.

ASSEMBLY

Serve the chicken mixture in bowls. Garnish with the lettuce, cheese, tomato, avocado and cilantro.

NOTE *You can also use 1 can (19 oz/540 ml) small black beans, rinsed and drained.*

PREPARATION	PRESSURE COOKING	SERVINGS
15 MIN	10 MIN	4 TO 6

PRESSURIZATION	DEPRESSURIZATION	FREEZES
15 MIN	MANUAL	–

HIBACHI-STYLE FRIED RICE

6	green onions, thinly sliced, white and green parts separated
2	garlic cloves, finely chopped
1 tbsp	finely chopped fresh ginger
2 tbsp	(30 ml) vegetable oil
1½ cups	(320 g) sushi rice (Calrose), rinsed well and drained
1¼ cups	(310 ml) chicken broth (recipe p. 8)
2 tbsp	(30 ml) soy sauce
1 tbsp	(15 ml) toasted sesame oil
2 cups	(290 g) frozen shelled edamame, thawed
1 tsp	(5 ml) sambal oelek
2	eggs, lightly beaten

Preheat the container of your pressure cooker on the Sauté function for 2 minutes. Soften the white parts of the green onions, garlic and ginger in the vegetable oil for 2 minutes. Add the rice and stir to coat well.

Add the broth and soy sauce. Secure the lid and set to High pressure. Set the cooking time to 10 minutes.

When ready, depressurize your pressure cooker manually, then remove the lid. Select the Sauté function. Add the sesame oil and brown the rice, cooking for 8 to 10 minutes, stirring regularly.

Add the edamame, sambal oelek and eggs, stirring constantly until the eggs are cooked. Add the green parts of the green onions. Adjust the seasoning.

NOTE *To vary, you can add shrimp or pulled chicken (recipe p. 61) at the same time as the edamame.*

PREPARATION	PRESSURE COOKING	SERVINGS
30 MIN	10 MIN	4

PRESSURIZATION	DEPRESSURIZATION	FREEZES
5 MIN	MANUAL	–

THE SECRET? ONCE THE RICE IS COOKED, PRESS "SAUTÉ" TO GIVE IT SOME COLOR.

LENTIL AND POTATO CURRY

1	large onion, finely chopped
2	garlic cloves, finely chopped
2 tbsp	ghee or butter
1 tbsp	garam masala
1 tsp	turmeric
½ tsp	ground cumin
3 cups	(750 ml) chicken broth (recipe p. 8)
4 cups	(680 g) unpeeled red potatoes, cut into large cubes
1½ cups	(300 g) dried green lentils, rinsed and drained
1 can	(14 oz/398 ml) coconut milk
	Cilantro leaves, to taste

Preheat the container of your pressure cooker on the Sauté function for 2 minutes. Brown the onion and garlic in the ghee. Add the spices and cook for 1 minute, stirring.

Add the broth, potatoes and lentils. Season with salt and pepper and mix well. Secure the lid and select the Bean function (or set to High pressure). Set the cooking time to 10 minutes.

When ready, depressurize your pressure cooker manually, then remove the lid. Add the coconut milk and stir gently. Adjust the seasoning. Sprinkle with the cilantro. Serve with basmati rice, if desired.

PREPARATION	PRESSURE COOKING	SERVINGS
20 MIN	10 MIN	4 TO 6
PRESSURIZATION	**DEPRESSURIZATION**	**FREEZES**
15 MIN	MANUAL	YES

BIRYANI-INSPIRED CHICKEN AND RICE CASSEROLE

MARINATED CHICKEN

1½ lb	(675 g) bone-in, skinless chicken thighs
3	garlic cloves, finely chopped
¼ cup	(60 ml) plain yogurt
1 tbsp	finely chopped fresh ginger
1 tbsp	garam masala
1 tsp	(5 ml) sambal oelek

CASSEROLE

1	onion, thinly sliced
2 tbsp	ghee or butter
5	cardamom pods
2	cloves
1	cinnamon stick 2 inches (5 cm) long
1	star anise
1	pinch saffron (8 to 10 threads)
1½ cups	(285 g) basmati rice, rinsed well and drained
1½ cups	(375 ml) chicken broth (recipe p. 8)

MARINATED CHICKEN

In a bowl, combine the chicken with the remaining ingredients. Cover and let marinate in the refrigerator for 1 to 12 hours.

CASSEROLE

Preheat the container of your pressure cooker on the Sauté function for 2 minutes. Brown the onion in the ghee along with the spices. Add half of the chicken at a time, browning it on each side. Season with salt.

Add the rice and broth. Mix well. Secure the lid and select the Poultry function (or set to High pressure). Set the cooking time to 10 minutes.

When ready, let your pressure cooker depressurize naturally (about 10 minutes), then remove the lid. Mix well. Cover and let rest for 5 minutes. Remove and compost the cardamom pods, cloves, cinnamon stick and star anise. Adjust the seasoning. Serve the casserole with a green vegetable, if desired.

PREPARATION	PRESSURIZATION	SERVINGS
25 MIN	10 MIN	4

MARINATING	PRESSURE COOKING	FREEZES
1 H	10 MIN	–

DEPRESSURIZATION
10 MIN

CHANA MASALA-STYLE CHICKPEAS AND SPINACH CURRY

2 cups	(410 g) dried chickpeas
1	onion, finely chopped
4	garlic cloves, finely chopped
1	piece fresh ginger 1 inch (2.5 cm) long, peeled
1	whole bird's eye chili (optional)
2 tbsp	ghee or butter
4 tsp	curry powder
1 tsp	cumin seeds
1 can	(14 oz/398 ml) diced tomatoes
1 cup	(250 ml) vegetable or chicken broth (recipes p. 6 and p. 8)
6 cups	(140 g) baby spinach
2 tbsp	(30 ml) lemon juice

Place the chickpeas in a bowl. Cover with water and soak for 12 hours or overnight at room temperature. Add water as needed so that the chickpeas are always well covered. Rinse and drain.

Preheat the container of your pressure cooker on the Sauté function for 2 minutes. Brown the onion, garlic, ginger and chili in the ghee. Add the spices and cook for 1 minute, stirring.

Add the chickpeas, tomatoes and broth. Season with salt and pepper and mix well. Secure the lid and select the Bean function (or set to High pressure). Set the cooking time to 45 minutes.

When ready, depressurize your pressure cooker manually, then remove the lid. Remove and compost the ginger and chili. Stir in the spinach and lemon juice. Simmer for 2 minutes or until the spinach is just wilted. Adjust the seasoning.

PREPARATION	PRESSURIZATION	SERVINGS
20 MIN	5 MIN	4
SOAKING	**PRESSURE COOKING**	**FREEZES**
12 H	45 MIN	YES
	DEPRESSURIZATION	
	MANUAL	

biryani-inspired
chicken and
rice casserole
(page 82)

A FEW SPICES MAKE
FOR BIG FLAVOR.

chana masala-
style chickpeas
and spinach curry
(page 83)

HUMMUS

1 cup	(205 g) dried chickpeas
3	garlic cloves, peeled
¼ tsp	baking soda
3 cups	(750 ml) water
½ cup	(125 ml) tahini (sesame butter)
1	lemon, for juice
½ tsp	salt
½ tsp	ground cumin
	Olive oil, to taste
	Finely chopped flat-leaf parsley, to taste
	Roasted cumin seeds, to taste
	Roasted sesame seeds, to taste
	Ground sumac, to taste

Place the chickpeas in a bowl. Cover with water and soak for 12 hours or overnight at room temperature. Add water as needed so that the chickpeas are always well covered. Rinse and drain.

In the container of the pressure cooker, combine the chickpeas, garlic, baking soda and water. Secure the lid and set to Low pressure. Set the cooking time to 25 minutes.

When ready, depressurize your pressure cooker manually, then remove the lid. Drain the chickpeas and garlic. Let cool.

In a food processor, purée the chickpeas with the garlic, tahini, lemon juice, salt and ground cumin until smooth. Using a spatula, scrape the sides of the food processor a few times. Add water, if needed, to achieve the desired consistency.

Transfer to a serving bowl. Drizzle with the oil. Garnish with the parsley, cumin and sesame seeds and sumac. Serve as a dip, with wedges of fresh or toasted pita, or as an accompaniment to grilled meat or poultry.

PREPARATION	PRESSURIZATION	MAKES
15 MIN	10 MIN	2½ CUPS (625 ML)
SOAKING	**PRESSURE COOKING**	**FREEZES**
12 H	25 MIN	–
	DEPRESSURIZATION	
	MANUAL	

WILD RICE READY IN
35 MINUTES RATHER THAN
IN AN HOUR? WE LOVE IT!

CHICKEN AND WILD RICE SALAD PITAS

½ cup	(100 g) wild rice, rinsed well and drained
¼ cup	(40 g) dried cranberries, coarsely chopped
¾ cup	(180 ml) water
2 cups	(340 g) pulled chicken (recipe p. 61)
¼ cup	(60 ml) sour cream
2 tbsp	(30 ml) mayonnaise
2 tbsp	finely chopped chives
2	pitas, 8 inches (20 cm) in diameter, halved
	Boston lettuce leaves, to taste

In the container of the pressure cooker, combine the rice, cranberries and water. Secure the lid and set to High pressure. Set the cooking time to 35 minutes.

When ready, depressurize your pressure cooker manually, then remove the lid. Mix well to fluff the rice. Cover and let rest for 5 minutes. Let cool.

In a bowl, combine the cranberry rice, chicken, sour cream, mayonnaise and chives. Season with salt and pepper.

Gently open the pita halves. Fill with the wild rice chicken salad and lettuce.

PREPARATION	PRESSURE COOKING	SERVINGS
20 MIN	35 MIN	4

PRESSURIZATION	DEPRESSURIZATION	FREEZES
5 MIN	MANUAL	–

PEA RISOTTO

½ cup   (60 g) chopped shallots
¼ cup   (55 g) butter
1½ cups (315 g) arborio rice
½ cup   (125 ml) white wine
3 cups   (750 ml) chicken broth (recipe p. 8)
1½ cups (225 g) frozen peas, thawed
1 cup   (70 g) grated fresh Parmesan cheese

Preheat the pressure cooker container on the Sauté function for 2 minutes. Soften the shallots in the butter for 2 minutes. Add the rice and cook for 1 minute, stirring to coat well.

Deglaze with the wine and cook, stirring, for 2 minutes or until the liquid is almost completely evaporated. Add the broth. Secure the lid and select the Soup function (or set to High pressure). Set the cooking time to 6 minutes.

When ready, depressurize your pressure cooker manually, then remove the lid. Add the peas and ½ cup (35 g) of cheese. Mix well. Cover and let rest for 2 minutes. Adjust the seasoning.

Divide the risotto among four bowls. Garnish with the remaining ½ cup (35 g) of cheese.

PREPARATION	PRESSURE COOKING	SERVINGS
25 MIN	6 MIN	4
PRESSURIZATION	**DEPRESSURIZATION**	**FREEZES**
5 MIN	MANUAL	–

A RISOTTO MADE IN A
PRESSURE COOKER? YES!

MAPLE BAKED BEANS

2¼ cups (450 g) dried small white beans or navy beans
1½ cups (375 ml) water
½ cup (125 ml) maple syrup
¼ cup (60 ml) ketchup
¼ cup (60 ml) molasses
2 slices bacon, cut into 4 pieces
1 onion, quartered
1 tsp dry mustard
½ tsp salt
¼ tsp ground pepper

Place the beans in a bowl. Cover with water and let soak for 12 hours or overnight at room temperature. Add water as needed so that the beans are always well covered. Rinse and drain.

In the container of your pressure cooker, combine all the ingredients. Secure the lid and select the Bean function (or set to High pressure). Set the cooking time to 60 minutes.

When ready, depressurize your pressure cooker manually, then remove the lid. Mix well. Cover and let rest for 5 minutes. Adjust the seasoning.

PREPARATION	PRESSURIZATION	SERVINGS
20 MIN	15 MIN	4 TO 6
SOAKING	**PRESSURE COOKING**	**FREEZES**
12 H	60 MIN	YES
	DEPRESSURIZATION	
	MANUAL	

beef bourguignon (page 120)

A COMFORT CLASSIC.

SAUCES & STEWS

We bring together many classics in this section. Beef Stroganoff and bourguignon, beef braised in carrot juice, spaghetti sauces, chili . . . These familiar, friendly dishes are all ideal for the pressure cooker. Tougher cuts of meat will find their happy place in the appliance, which makes them fall-apart tender. Thanks to the pressure cooker, these comfort meals are only a press of a button away!

WHETHER YOU PREFER A CLASSIC OR VEGETARIAN SPAGHETTI SAUCE, WITH THE PRESSURE COOKER YOU DON'T NEED TO LET IT SIMMER FOR HOURS ON THE STOVETOP. YOU CAN JUST TOSS IN THE INGREDIENTS, SEAL THE LID AND ENJOY A FLAVORFUL SAUCE IN RECORD TIME.

SPAGHETTI SAUCE WITH MEAT

¾ lb	(340 g) mild or spicy Italian sausage meat (3 to 4 sausages)
2 tbsp	(30 ml) olive oil
¾ lb	(340 g) lean ground beef
1	large onion, finely chopped
2	carrots, diced
2	stalks celery, diced
2	garlic cloves, finely chopped
1 can	(28 oz/796 ml) diced plum tomatoes
1 can	(28 oz/796 ml) tomato sauce or crushed tomatoes with purée
1 tsp	dried oregano
1	clove
¼ cup	(60 ml) tomato paste

Preheat the container of your pressure cooker on the Sauté function for 2 minutes. Brown the sausage meat in 1 tbsp (15 ml) of oil, breaking it apart with a wooden spoon.

Meanwhile, in a large skillet over high heat, brown the ground beef in the remaining 1 tbsp (15 ml) of oil (see note), breaking it apart with a wooden spoon. Season with salt and pepper. Add the onion, carrots, celery and garlic. Cook for 2 minutes, stirring. Transfer to the pressure cooker.

Add the tomatoes, tomato sauce, oregano and clove. Stir to thoroughly combine. Season with salt and pepper. Add the tomato paste, without mixing it in. Secure the lid and select the Meat function (or set to High pressure). Set the cooking time to 30 minutes.

When ready, let your pressure cooker depressurize naturally (about 15 minutes), then remove the lid. Mix well. Adjust the seasoning. Remove and compost the clove. Serve over pasta of your choice.

NOTE *You can also brown the beef in the container of the pressure cooker. Set the cooked sausage meat aside on a plate, then add it to the pressure cooker at the same time as the tomatoes.*

PREPARATION	PRESSURE COOKING	MAKES
40 MIN	30 MIN	10 CUPS (2.5 L)
PRESSURIZATION	**DEPRESSURIZATION**	**FREEZES**
20 MIN	15 MIN	YES

MEATLESS SPAGHETTI SAUCE

10	garlic cloves, chopped
2	onions, chopped
2 tbsp	(30 ml) olive oil
½ lb	(225 g) white mushrooms, chopped
1 cup	(250 ml) red wine
2	stalks celery, chopped
2	carrots, diced
1½ cups	(150 g) textured vegetable protein (TVP) in small flakes (see note)

2 cans	(28 oz/796 ml each) diced plum tomatoes
1 cup	(250 ml) vegetable broth (recipe p. 6) or mushroom broth
2 tsp	ground pickling spice
1½ tsp	ground fennel seeds
1 tsp	dried oregano
1 tsp	red pepper flakes
1	bay leaf
2 tbsp	(30 ml) tomato paste

Preheat the container of your pressure cooker on the Sauté function for 2 minutes. Brown the garlic and onions in the oil. Add the mushrooms and brown them for 5 minutes. Deglaze with the wine and let reduce for 2 minutes.

Add the remaining ingredients except for the tomato paste. Season with salt and pepper. Add the tomato paste, without mixing it in. Secure the lid and select the Soup function (or set to High pressure). Set the cooking time to 22 minutes.

When ready, let your pressure cooker depressurize naturally (about 15 minutes), then remove the lid. Mix well (see note). Adjust the seasoning. Remove the bay leaf and compost. Serve over pasta of your choice.

NOTES *You will find TVP in most health food stores and, increasingly, in supermarkets.*

You can select the Sauté function and simmer for 10 minutes so that the cooking juice evaporates and the sauce thickens. It will be thicker the following day, after a night in the refrigerator.

PREPARATION	PRESSURE COOKING	MAKES
40 MIN	22 MIN	10 CUPS (2.5 L)
PRESSURIZATION	**DEPRESSURIZATION**	**FREEZES**
10 MIN	15 MIN	YES

BRAISED BEEF
IN CARROT JUICE

2 lb	(900 g) boneless beef blade roast, cut into 6 slices
1	onion, halved
3 tbsp	(45 ml) olive oil
1½ cups	(375 ml) carrot juice
6	carrots, cut into rounds ½ inch (1 cm) thick
4	garlic cloves, chopped
1	leek, white part only, cut into pieces 1 inch (2.5 cm) long
1	stalk celery, cut into pieces 1 inch (2.5 cm) long
1	bay leaf
2 tbsp	finely chopped flat-leaf parsley

Preheat the container of your pressure cooker on the Sauté function for 2 minutes. Brown the meat and onion in the oil. Season with salt and pepper.

Add the remaining ingredients except for the parsley. Secure the lid and select the Meat function (or set to High pressure). Set the cooking time to 45 minutes.

When ready, let your pressure cooker depressurize naturally (about 15 minutes), then remove the lid. Remove the bay leaf and compost. Adjust the seasoning. Garnish with the parsley. Serve the braised beef with mashed potatoes, if desired.

PREPARATION	PRESSURE COOKING	SERVINGS
30 MIN	45 MIN	5

PRESSURIZATION	DEPRESSURIZATION	FREEZES
10 MIN	15 MIN	–

TIKKA MASALA-INSPIRED LAMB

1	red onion, finely chopped
4	garlic cloves, finely chopped
1 tbsp	finely chopped fresh ginger
2 tbsp	ghee or butter
1 tbsp	garam masala
1 tbsp	chili powder
1	pinch ground cinnamon
1½ lb	(675 g) lamb shoulder, cubed
¼ cup	(35 g) ground almonds
¾ cup	(180 ml) 35% cream
2 tbsp	(30 ml) tomato paste
	Plain yogurt (optional)
	Cilantro leaves (optional)

Preheat the container of your pressure cooker on the Sauté function for 2 minutes. Brown the onion, garlic and ginger in the ghee. Add the spices and cook, stirring, for 1 minute.

Add the meat, ground almonds, cream and tomato paste. Season with salt and pepper and mix well. Secure the lid and select the Soup function (or set to High pressure). Set the cooking time to 7 minutes.

When ready, let your pressure cooker depressurize naturally (about 10 minutes), then remove the lid. Adjust the seasoning. Garnish the tikka masala with plain yogurt and cilantro. Serve with basmati rice and naan, if desired.

PREPARATION	PRESSURE COOKING	SERVINGS
20 MIN	7 MIN	4
PRESSURIZATION	**DEPRESSURIZATION**	**FREEZES**
5 MIN	10 MIN	-

CARAMEL PORK STEW

2.2 lb	(1 kg) boneless pork shoulder roast without the rind, cut into 6 slices
3 tbsp	(45 ml) vegetable oil
2	onions, thinly sliced
4	garlic cloves, chopped
1 tbsp	chopped fresh ginger
3 tbsp	brown sugar
1 cup	(250 ml) coconut milk
3 tbsp	(45 ml) fish sauce
1 tbsp	(15 ml) soy sauce
6	hard-boiled eggs (recipe p. 146) (optional)

Preheat the container of your pressure cooker on the Sauté function for 2 minutes. Brown the meat in the oil. Set aside on a plate.

Brown the onions. Add the garlic and ginger and cook for 1 minute. Add the brown sugar and cook until caramelized. Add the coconut milk, fish sauce and soy sauce. Mix well. Return the meat to the pressure cooker. Secure the lid and select the Meat function (or set to High pressure). Set the cooking time to 40 minutes.

When ready, let your pressure cooker depressurize naturally (about 15 minutes), then remove the lid. Mix well. Adjust the seasoning. Select the Sauté function. Bring the stew to a boil. Add the boiled eggs, and cook for 2 minutes. Serve the stew with basmati rice, if desired.

PREPARATION	PRESSURE COOKING	SERVINGS
30 MIN	40 MIN	4 TO 6

PRESSURIZATION	DEPRESSURIZATION	FREEZES
5 MIN	15 MIN	–

RICARDO'S
FAVORITE!

PORK SATAY

2.2 lb	(1 kg) boneless pork shoulder roast without the rind, cubed
3 tbsp	(45 ml) vegetable oil
6	green onions, thinly sliced, white and green parts separated
2	garlic cloves, finely chopped
1 tbsp	finely chopped fresh ginger
1 cup	(250 ml) chicken broth (recipe p. 8)
¼ cup	(60 ml) lime juice
¼ cup	(60 ml) soy sauce
1 tbsp	(15 ml) honey
2 tsp	(10 ml) sambal oelek, or more to taste
¾ cup	(180 ml) peanut butter
½ cup	(125 ml) 10% plain yogurt
¼ cup	(40 g) unsalted roasted peanuts, chopped
⅓ cup	(15 g) finely chopped cilantro

Preheat the container of your pressure cooker on the Sauté function for 2 minutes. Brown half of the meat at a time in the oil. Season with salt and pepper. Toward the end of cooking, add the white parts of the green onions, garlic and ginger. Cook for 2 minutes, stirring.

Add the broth, lime juice, soy sauce, honey and sambal oelek. Mix well. Secure the lid and select the Meat function (or set to High pressure). Set the cooking time to 25 minutes.

When ready, let your pressure cooker depressurize naturally (about 15 minutes), then remove the lid. Take 1 cup (250 ml) of cooking juice and pour it into a bowl. Add the peanut butter and mix well with a whisk. Transfer to the pressure cooker along with the green parts of the green onions. Mix well. Adjust the seasoning.

Serve the pork satay in bowls, over basmati rice, if desired. Top with the yogurt, peanuts and cilantro.

PREPARATION	PRESSURE COOKING	SERVINGS
40 MIN	25 MIN	4 TO 6

PRESSURIZATION	DEPRESSURIZATION	FREEZES
5 MIN	15 MIN	–

CHICKEN STEW WITH PRUNES AND SPINACH

1½ lb	(675 g) boneless, skinless chicken thighs, cut into 2 or 3 pieces
2 tbsp	(30 ml) vegetable oil
1	onion, chopped
2	garlic cloves, chopped
½ tsp	turmeric
⅛ tsp	ground cinnamon
1 cup	(250 ml) chicken broth (recipe p. 8)
1 cup	(200 g) pitted prunes
12 cups	(280 g) baby spinach, coarsely chopped

Preheat the container of your pressure cooker on the Sauté function for 2 minutes. Brown the chicken in the oil. Season with salt and pepper. Add the onion and garlic. Cook for 2 minutes, stirring.

Add the remaining ingredients except for the spinach. Secure the lid and select the Poultry function (or set to High pressure). Set the cooking time to 10 minutes.

When ready, let your pressure cooker depressurize naturally (about 10 minutes), then remove the lid. Stir in the spinach. Cover and let rest for 2 minutes or until the spinach has wilted. Adjust the seasoning. Serve the stew with rice pilaf (without the currants) (recipe p. 74) or basmati rice, if desired.

PREPARATION	PRESSURE COOKING	SERVINGS
20 MIN	10 MIN	4
PRESSURIZATION	**DEPRESSURIZATION**	**FREEZES**
5 MIN	10 MIN	–

TRY THIS VERSION
COOKED IN BEER AND
MAPLE SYRUP: IT'LL MELT
IN YOUR MOUTH!

MAPLE AND BEER HAM

1	bone-in smoked ham shoulder, approximately 5 ½ lb (2.5 kg)
2 tbsp	(30 ml) Dijon mustard
3	cloves
1	bottle or can (12 oz/355 ml) pale ale
½ cup	(125 ml) maple syrup
	Cold water

Remove the string from the ham. Place the ham in the container of your pressure cooker, cut-side down. Brush with the mustard and prick with the cloves.

Pour the beer and maple syrup overtop. Pour the water in up to the maximum level of the container of the pressure cooker (four-fifths of the way). Secure the lid and select the Meat function (or set to High pressure). Set the cooking time to 45 minutes.

When ready, let your pressure cooker depressurize naturally (about 15 minutes), then remove the lid.

Remove the ham from the container. Slice it into pieces. Reserve the cooking juice to cook potatoes, if desired (see note).

NOTE *Place peeled potatoes of approximately the same size as each other in the ham cooking juice. Secure the lid and select the Root vegetable function (or set to High pressure). Set the cooking time to 15 minutes. When ready, depressurize your pressure cooker manually, then remove the lid.*

PREPARATION	PRESSURE COOKING	SERVINGS
10 MIN	45 MIN	10

PRESSURIZATION	DEPRESSURIZATION	FREEZES
25 MIN	15 MIN	–

VEGGIE CHILI WITH BLACK BEANS

1½ cups	(300 g) dried small black beans
2	onions, chopped
3	garlic cloves, chopped
1	jalapeño pepper, seeded or not, finely chopped
2 tbsp	(30 ml) olive oil
3 tbsp	chili powder
1 can	(28 oz/796 ml) diced tomatoes
1 cup	(250 ml) vegetable broth (recipe p. 6)
1	red bell pepper, seeded and diced
2 cups	(300 g) diced peeled sweet potatoes
1½ cups	(225 g) frozen corn kernels
½ cup	(75 g) roasted peanuts, finely chopped
⅓ cup	(15 g) finely chopped cilantro

Place the beans in a bowl. Cover with water and soak for 12 hours or overnight at room temperature. Add water as needed so that the beans are always well covered. Rinse and drain.

Preheat the container of your pressure cooker on the Sauté function for 2 minutes. Brown the onions, garlic and jalapeño in the oil. Add the chili powder and cook for 1 minute, stirring.

Add the black beans, tomatoes and broth. Season with salt and pepper and mix well. Secure the lid and select the Bean function (or set to High pressure). Set the cooking time to 25 minutes.

When ready, depressurize your pressure cooker manually, then remove the lid. Add the bell pepper, sweet potatoes and corn. Mix well. Secure the lid and select the Root vegetable function (or set to High pressure). Set the cooking time to 6 minutes.

When ready, depressurize your pressure cooker manually, then remove the lid. Mix well. Adjust the seasoning. Top with the peanuts and cilantro.

PREPARATION	PRESSURIZATION	SERVINGS
30 MIN	15 MIN	4 TO 6
SOAKING	**PRESSURE COOKING**	**FREEZES**
12 H	31 MIN	YES
	DEPRESSURIZATION	
	MANUAL	

CLASSIC OR VEGETARIAN, WHO DOESN'T LOVE CHILI? ESPECIALLY WITH THESE SHORT COOK TIMES!

CLASSIC BEEF CHILI

1 cup	(200 g) dried small red beans
1	onion, finely chopped
1	jalapeño pepper, seeded or not, finely chopped
2 tbsp	butter
2 lb	(900 g) lean ground beef
2	garlic cloves, finely chopped
1 can	(28 oz/796 ml) diced tomatoes
1 cup	(250 ml) strong coffee or beef broth (recipe p. 9)
¼ cup	(60 ml) ketchup
3 tbsp	(45 ml) lime juice
2 tbsp	chili powder
1 tsp	ground cumin
¼ cup	(10 g) finely chopped cilantro (optional)

Place the beans in a bowl. Cover with water and soak for 12 hours or overnight at room temperature. Add water as needed so that the beans are always well covered. Rinse and drain.

Preheat the container of your pressure cooker on the Sauté function for 2 minutes. Brown the onion and jalapeño in the butter. Add the beef and garlic. Cook the meat, breaking it apart with a wooden spoon, until golden. Season with salt and pepper.

Add the remaining ingredients except for the cilantro. Season with salt and pepper. Secure the lid and select the Bean function (or set to High pressure). Set the cooking time to 25 minutes.

When ready, depressurize your pressure cooker manually, then remove the lid. Mix well. Adjust the seasoning. Sprinkle with the cilantro.

PREPARATION	PRESSURIZATION	SERVINGS
35 MIN	10 MIN	4 TO 6
SOAKING	**PRESSURE COOKING**	**FREEZES**
12 H	25 MIN	YES
	DEPRESSURIZATION	
	MANUAL	

BEEF STROGANOFF

1½ lb	(675 g) steak or sirloin beef roast, cut into strips
2 tbsp	(30 ml) olive oil, plus more for the noodles
2	onions, thinly sliced
3	garlic cloves, chopped
1 lb	(450 g) small white mushrooms
2 tbsp	butter
2 tbsp	unbleached all-purpose flour
½ cup	(125 ml) red wine
1 cup	(250 ml) beef broth (recipe p. 9)
2 tbsp	(30 ml) whole-grain mustard
1 tsp	sweet paprika
½ lb	(225 g) egg noodles
¾ cup	(180 ml) 10% plain yogurt
¼ cup	(10 g) finely chopped chives

In a large non-stick skillet over medium-high heat, brown one-third of the meat at a time in the oil (see note). Season with salt and pepper.

Meanwhile, preheat the container of your pressure cooker on the Sauté function for 2 minutes. Cook the onions, garlic and mushrooms in the butter until they begin to brown. Sprinkle with the flour and cook for 1 minute, stirring. Season with salt and pepper. Deglaze with the wine.

Add the broth, mustard, paprika and browned meat. Mix well. Secure the lid and select the Meat function (or set to High pressure). Set the cooking time to 25 minutes.

In a pot of salted boiling water, cook the noodles until al dente. Drain. Lightly oil the noodles.

When ready, let your pressure cooker depressurize naturally (about 15 minutes), then remove the lid. Stir in the yogurt. Adjust the seasoning. Sprinkle with the chives. Serve over the egg noodles.

NOTE *You can brown the meat in the container of the pressure cooker, but you will have to do it in three batches before the aromatics, which lengthens the cooking time. By browning the meat in a skillet at the same time as the aromatics in the container, you save time.*

PREPARATION	PRESSURE COOKING	SERVINGS
35 MIN	25 MIN	4 TO 6

PRESSURIZATION	DEPRESSURIZATION	FREEZES
5 MIN	15 MIN	–

BOLOGNESE

2 oz	(55 g) pancetta, finely chopped
1 lb	(450 g) lean ground meat (a mix of veal, beef and pork)
2 tbsp	butter
1	onion, finely chopped
2	carrots, grated
2	stalks celery, finely chopped
2	garlic cloves, finely chopped
¼ cup	(60 ml) white or red wine
1 cup	(250 ml) beef broth (recipe p. 9)
¼ cup	(60 ml) 35% cream
¼ cup	(60 ml) tomato paste

In a large non-stick skillet over medium-high heat, brown the pancetta and ground meat in 1 tbsp of butter, breaking apart the ground meat with a wooden spoon (see note). Season with salt and pepper.

Meanwhile, preheat the container of your pressure cooker on the Sauté function for 2 minutes. Brown the onion, carrots, celery and garlic in the remaining 1 tbsp of butter. Season with salt and pepper. Add the meat mixture. Deglaze with the wine and cook for 1 minute, stirring. Stir in the broth and cream. Add the tomato paste, without mixing it in. Secure the lid and select the Meat function (or set to High pressure). Set the cooking time to 20 minutes.

When ready, let your pressure cooker depressurize naturally (about 15 minutes), then remove the lid. Mix well. Adjust the seasoning. Serve over the pasta of your choice.

NOTE *You can also brown the pancetta and ground meat in the container of the pressure cooker. Then set them aside on a plate and brown the vegetables.*

PREPARATION	PRESSURE COOKING	MAKES
35 MIN	20 MIN	4 CUPS (1 L)

PRESSURIZATION	DEPRESSURIZATION	FREEZES
5 MIN	15 MIN	YES

BEEF BOURGUIGNON

½ lb	(225 g) white mushrooms, halved
¼ lb	(115 g) bacon, cut into large dice
1	carrot, cut into small dice
2 tbsp	butter
2.2 lb	(1 kg) boneless beef blade roast, fat removed, cubed
1	onion, chopped
1 cup	(250 ml) red wine
1 cup	(250 ml) beef broth (recipe p. 9)
3 tbsp	flour, lightly toasted
1 tbsp	(15 ml) tomato paste

Preheat the container of your pressure cooker on the Sauté function for 2 minutes. Brown the mushrooms, bacon and carrot in 1 tbsp of butter.

Meanwhile, in a large skillet over high heat, brown the beef in the remaining 1 tbsp of butter (see note). Season with salt and pepper. Add the onion and cook for 2 minutes. Deglaze with the wine. Transfer to the pressure cooker.

Add the remaining ingredients. Stir to thoroughly combine. Season with salt and pepper. Secure the lid and select the Meat function (or set to High pressure). Set the cooking time to 35 minutes.

When ready, let your pressure cooker depressurize naturally (about 15 minutes), then remove the lid. Adjust the seasoning. Serve with mashed potatoes, if desired.

NOTE *You can brown the meat in the container of your pressure cooker, but you will have to do it in two batches before the aromatics, which lengthens the cooking time. By browning the meat in a skillet at the same time as the aromatics in the container, you save time.*

PREPARATION	PRESSURE COOKING	SERVINGS
40 MIN	35 MIN	4

PRESSURIZATION	DEPRESSURIZATION	FREEZES
5 MIN	15 MIN	YES

A MEAT THAT COMES
APART WITH A FORK
IN 30 MINUTES?
WE PROMISE!

MEATBALL STEW

SAUCE

6 cups	(1.5 L) pork broth (recipe p. 7)
½ cup	(70 g) flour, lightly toasted
¼ cup	(40 g) unbleached all-purpose flour
¼ tsp	ground cinnamon
¼ tsp	ground clove
¾ cup	(180 ml) cold water

MEATBALLS

1½ lb	(675 g) lean ground pork
2	green onions, finely chopped
1	egg
⅓ cup	(40 g) breadcrumbs
3 tbsp	(45 ml) milk
1 tsp	dry mustard
¼ tsp	ground nutmeg
	Cooked pork shank meat from pork broth (recipe p. 7)

SAUCE

Preheat the container of your pressure cooker on the Sauté function for 2 minutes. Add the broth and simmer.

Meanwhile, in a bowl, combine the flours, cinnamon and clove. Add the water and whisk until the mixture is a smooth paste, adding more water as needed. Add this mixture to the broth, stirring with a whisk. Bring to a boil. Adjust the seasoning.

MEATBALLS

In a bowl, combine the pork with the green onions, egg, breadcrumbs, milk, mustard and nutmeg. Season with salt and pepper. With lightly oiled hands, shape meatballs using 1 tbsp (15 ml) of meat mixture per ball. Place them in the simmering sauce as you go.

Add the pork shank meat. Season with salt and pepper. Secure the lid and select the Soup function (or set to High pressure). Set the cooking time to 7 minutes.

When ready, let your pressure cooker depressurize naturally (about 15 minutes), then remove the lid. Adjust the seasoning. Serve the stew with steamed or mashed potatoes, if desired.

PREPARATION	PRESSURE COOKING	SERVINGS
35 MIN	7 MIN	6
PRESSURIZATION	**DEPRESSURIZATION**	**FREEZES**
10 MIN	15 MIN	YES

CREAMY VEAL STEW

2 lb	(900 g) veal shoulder, cubed		2 tbsp	cornstarch
3 tbsp	(45 ml) olive oil		½ cup	(125 ml) 35% cream
2	shallots, chopped		3	unpeeled red potatoes, cut into large cubes
2	garlic cloves, thinly sliced		3	carrots, peeled and cut into pieces 1 inch (2.5 cm) long
½ cup	(125 ml) white wine		2	white turnips, peeled and cut into wedges 1 inch (2.5 cm) thick
1½ cups	(375 ml) chicken broth (recipe p. 8)			
1	bay leaf			

Preheat the container of your pressure cooker on the Sauté function for 2 minutes. Brown half of the meat at a time in 2 tbsp (30 ml) of oil. Season with salt and pepper. Set aside on a plate.

Brown the shallots and garlic in the remaining 1 tbsp (15 ml) of oil. Deglaze with the wine and reduce by half. Add the broth and bay leaf. Add the meat. Secure the lid and select the Meat function (or set to High pressure). Set the cooking time to 15 minutes.

Meanwhile, in a bowl, combine the cornstarch and cream until smooth.

When ready, depressurize your pressure cooker manually, then remove the lid. Add the cream mixture and vegetables. Season with salt and pepper and mix well. Secure the lid and select the Root vegetable function (or set to High pressure). Set the cooking time to 10 minutes.

When ready, let your pressure cooker depressurize naturally (about 15 minutes), then remove the lid. Mix well. Remove and compost the bay leaf. Adjust the seasoning.

PREPARATION 35 MIN	**PRESSURE COOKING** 25 MIN	**SERVINGS** 4 TO 6
PRESSURIZATION 10 MIN	**DEPRESSURIZATION** 15 MIN	**FREEZES** –

MEAT AND VEGETABLES COOK AT THE SAME TIME SO THAT YOU CAN ENJOY A GLASS OF WINE IN THE MEANTIME!

BEEF STEW WITH PRUNES AND BEER

1	large onion, cut into 12 wedges
2 tbsp	butter
2 tbsp	(30 ml) olive oil
2 tbsp	unbleached all-purpose flour
2.2 lb	(1 kg) boneless beef blade roast, cubed
1 can	(15 oz/440 ml) black stout (Guinness-style)
1 cup	(250 ml) beef or chicken broth (recipes p. 9 and p. 8)
4	carrots, peeled and cut into 3 pieces each
4	potatoes, peeled and cut into 2 or 3 pieces each
1	medium turnip or small rutabaga, peeled and cut into 6 wedges
½ cup	(100 g) diced pitted prunes
¼ cup	(10 g) finely chopped flat-leaf parsley

Preheat the container of your pressure cooker on the Sauté function for 2 minutes. Brown the onion in 1 tbsp of butter and 1 tbsp (15 ml) of oil. Sprinkle with the flour and cook, stirring, for 1 minute.

Meanwhile, in a large skillet over high heat, brown the beef in two batches in the remaining 1 tbsp of butter and 1 tbsp of oil (see note). Season with salt and pepper. Deglaze with the beer. Transfer to the pressure cooker.

Add the remaining ingredients except for the parsley. Season with salt and pepper. Secure the lid and select the Meat function (or set to High pressure). Set the cooking time to 30 minutes.

When ready, let your pressure cooker depressurize naturally (about 15 minutes), then remove the lid. Adjust the seasoning. Garnish with the parsley.

NOTE *You can brown the meat in the container of the pressure cooker, but you will have to do it in two batches before the onion, which lengthens the cooking time. By browning the meat in a skillet at the same time as the onion in the container, you save time.*

PREPARATION	PRESSURE COOKING	SERVINGS
30 MIN	30 MIN	4 TO 6

PRESSURIZATION	DEPRESSURIZATION	FREEZES
10 MIN	15 MIN	–

WHY MAKE SEVERAL
PANCAKES WHEN YOU
CAN MAKE A GIANT
ONE TO SHARE!

giant pancake (page 144)

BREAKFASTS & SWEETS

There are many benefits of preparing breakfasts and sweets in the pressure cooker. For breakfast, you can delicately cook eggs, as well as prepare homemade dairy products such as yogurt and ricotta. As for sweets, we leave things that need to be baked to the oven and instead focus on soft, creamy desserts. The pressure cooker gives perfectly soft, uniform results, which are sought after in several sugary treats.

PLAIN YOGURT IN JARS

5 cups	(1.25 L) 3.25% milk
½ cup	(55 g) milk powder
1	packet (5 g) powdered yogurt culture starter

In a pot over medium-high heat, bring the milk and milk powder to a boil, stirring constantly. Transfer to a bowl and let cool for 1 hour at room temperature.

Stir in the yogurt culture. Place a sieve over a bowl and strain the mixture. Pour about ¾ cup (180 ml) into each of seven sterilized jars with a capacity of 1 cup (250 ml) each (see note). Close the jars and place them in the pressure cooker. Add water until the jars are covered halfway (about 3 cups/750 ml). Secure the lid and select the Yogurt function. Set the cooking time to 4 hours.

When ready, remove the lid of your pressure cooker. Remove the jars from the water and dry them with a clean dishcloth.

Refrigerate the jars for 4 hours. When ready to serve, garnish the yogurt with fresh fruit, jam or granola, if desired. Unopened jars of yogurt will keep for up to 2 weeks in the refrigerator.

NOTE *In order to fit all the jars in the container of the pressure cooker at the same time, use narrow, tall glass jars.*

PREPARATION	COOLING	FREEZES
25 MIN	5 H	–

COOKING	MAKES
4 H	7 (¾ CUP/180 ML) JARS, APPROX.

APPLESAUCE

4.4 lb (2 kg) McIntosh apples, cored and cubed (see note)
1 cup (250 ml) water
½ cup (105 g) sugar (optional)

Place the apples and water in the container of your pressure cooker. Secure the lid and set to High pressure. Set the cooking time to 5 minutes.

When ready, depressurize your pressure cooker manually, then remove the lid.

In a blender, purée the apples in two batches until smooth, with half the sugar added to each batch. The applesauce will keep for up to 3 weeks in an airtight container in the refrigerator.

NOTE *To get a beautiful pink color, do not peel the apples. This will also retain the skins' nutrients. For a light-colored sauce, peel the apples.*

PREPARATION	PRESSURE COOKING	MAKES
25 MIN	5 MIN	7 CUPS (1.75 L)

PRESSURIZATION	DEPRESSURIZATION	FREEZES
15 MIN	MANUAL	YES

COCONUT RICE PUDDING
WITH MANGO SAUCE

RICE PUDDING

¾ cup	(160 g)	arborio rice
½ cup	(105 g)	sugar
1½ cups	(375 ml)	milk, plus more as needed (see note)
1 can	(14 oz/398 ml)	coconut milk
1		cinnamon stick 2 inches (5 cm) long

MANGO SAUCE

2 cups	(280 g)	fresh or thawed frozen mango cubes
3 tbsp		sugar

RICE PUDDING

In the container of your pressure cooker, combine all the ingredients. Secure the lid and set to Low pressure. Set the cooking time to 12 minutes.

When ready, let your pressure cooker depressurize naturally (about 10 minutes), then remove the lid. Mix well. Transfer to a bowl and cover the surface of the rice pudding directly with plastic wrap. Let cool, then refrigerate until completely chilled, about 4 hours.

MANGO SAUCE

Meanwhile, in a blender, purée the mango cubes until smooth, adding water as needed. Add the sugar and process until dissolved. Strain through a sieve for an extra smooth purée, if desired. Refrigerate until needed.

Remove and compost the cinnamon stick from the rice pudding. Mix well (see note). Add milk, if needed, to achieve the desired consistency. Divide the rice pudding among six small bowls. Using a spoon, make a shallow crevice on the top of the pudding and swirl in the mango sauce.

NOTES *You can replace cow's milk with an almond or soy alternative for a dairy-free recipe.*

Depending on the fat content of the coconut milk, it might form a layer of fat on the surface of the pudding. Remove before mixing.

PREPARATION	PRESSURE COOKING	SERVINGS
10 MIN	12 MIN	6

PRESSURIZATION	DEPRESSURIZATION	FREEZES
10 MIN	10 MIN	–

REFRIGERATION
4 H

STICKY TOFFEE PUDDING

CAKE

¼ cup	(60 ml) water
¾ cup	(130 g) pitted and diced dates
¼ tsp	baking soda
1 cup	(150 g) unbleached all-purpose flour

1 tsp	baking powder
¼ cup	(55 g) unsalted or semi-salted butter, softened
¼ cup	(55 g) brown sugar
1	egg
¼ cup	(60 ml) milk

CARAMEL SAUCE

¾ cup	(180 ml) 35% cream
¾ cup	(160 g) brown sugar

CAKE

Butter a 6-inch (15 cm) springform pan (see note).

In a small pot, bring the water and dates to a boil. Add the baking soda and mix well. Remove from the heat and let cool at room temperature before adding it to the batter.

In a bowl, combine the flour and baking powder.

In another bowl, cream the butter with the brown sugar using an electric mixer. Add the egg and mix until smooth. With the machine running on low speed, add the dry ingredients, alternating with the milk, then add the date mixture, mixing until combined. Pour the batter into the prepared pan.

Prepare a water bath in the pressure cooker: pour 1 ½ cups (375 ml) of water into the container of your pressure cooker and add the silicone grill. Place the springform pan on the grill (see note). Secure the lid and set to High pressure. Set the cooking time to 25 minutes.

CARAMEL SAUCE

Meanwhile, in a small pot, bring the cream and brown sugar to a boil. Simmer for 2 minutes. Set aside.

When ready, let your pressure cooker depressurize naturally (about 10 minutes), then remove the lid.

Remove the pan from the cooker. Use a clean dishcloth to gently absorb any water that may have settled on the surface of the pudding. Using a toothpick, prick the entire surface and pour the sauce overtop. Let cool before unmolding, at least 30 minutes. Serve warm or cold.

NOTES *The RICARDO 6-inch silicone mould can be used for this sticky toffee pudding, and you won't have to butter it. However, if you do that, we suggest not unmolding the pudding, but rather using a spoon to serve it.*

If you don't have a silicone grill, make a coil with an 18-inch (45 cm) long sheet of foil. Place at the bottom of the container. Set the pan on top of the coil, making sure it doesn't touch the water and that it is straight.

PREPARATION	PRESSURE COOKING	SERVINGS
30 MIN	25 MIN	6

PRESSURIZATION	DEPRESSURIZATION	FREEZES
5 MIN	10 MIN	–

DULCE DE LECHE

1 can   **(10 oz/300 ml) sweetened condensed milk**

Pour the condensed milk into a Mason jar with a capacity of 2 cups (500 ml). Close the lid without tightening it all the way.

Place the jar in the container of your pressure cooker and pour water up to the height of the condensed milk. Secure the lid and set to High pressure. Set the cooking time to 45 minutes.

When ready, let your pressure cooker depressurize naturally (about 15 minutes), then remove the lid. Remove the jar from the water and place it on a dishcloth. Let cool. Delicious on cake. An unopened jar will keep for 6 months at room temperature. An opened jar will keep for 1 month in the refrigerator. Mix well before use.

NOTES *You can easily double or triple this recipe. Just use 1 can of condensed milk per jar. The cooking time will remain the same.*

For a salted caramel variation, add a pinch of fleur de sel to the condensed milk before pouring it into the jar and mix well.

PREPARATION	PRESSURE COOKING	MAKES
5 MIN	45 MIN	1¼ CUPS (310 ML), APPROX.

PRESSURIZATION	DEPRESSURIZATION	FREEZES
20 MIN	15 MIN	–

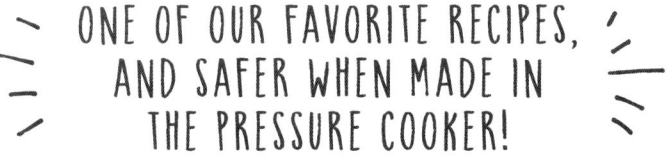

ONE OF OUR FAVORITE RECIPES, AND SAFER WHEN MADE IN THE PRESSURE COOKER!

THIS CAKE IS ULTRA-CREAMY IN THE PRESSURE COOKER, WITH NOT ONE DRY CRUMB. PERFECTION!

CHEESECAKE

CRUST		FILLING		½ cup	(125 ml) sour cream
¾ cup	(95 g) graham cracker crumbs	¾ cup	(160 g) sugar	2	blocks (9 oz/250 g) each cream cheese, softened
2 tbsp	butter, melted	1 tbsp	tapioca flour or unbleached all-purpose flour (see note)		
1 tbsp	brown sugar			2	egg yolks
				1	egg

CRUST

Line the bottom of a 6-inch (15 cm) springform pan with parchment paper. Line the sides with a strip of parchment paper (see note).

In a bowl, combine the graham cracker crumbs with the butter and brown sugar until the crumbs are moistened. Pack lightly along the bottom and one-third of the way up the sides of the pan. Place in the freezer for 15 minutes while preparing the filling.

FILLING

In a food processor, combine the sugar and tapioca flour. Add the sour cream and cream cheese. Process until the mixture is smooth, scraping the sides a few times with a spatula. Add the egg yolks and egg, and process again to combine. Pour the filling into the chilled crust.

Prepare a water bath in the pressure cooker: pour 1 cup (250 ml) of water into the container of your pressure cooker and add the silicone grill. Place the springform pan on the grill (see note). Secure the lid and set to High pressure. Set the cooking time to 32 minutes.

When ready, let your pressure cooker depressurize naturally (about 10 minutes), then remove the lid. Remove the pan from the cooker. Use a clean dishcloth to gently absorb any water that may have settled on the surface of the cake. Let cool for 1 hour. Cover and refrigerate for 4 hours or until completely chilled.

Unmold the cake. Remove the parchment paper. Cut into wedges and serve. Delicious with strawberries.

NOTES *Tapioca flour gives the cake a creamier texture.*

The RICARDO 6-inch silicone mould can also be used for baking the cheesecake.

If you don't have a silicone grill, make a coil with an 18-inch (45 cm) long sheet of foil. Place at the bottom of the container. Set the pan on top of the coil, making sure it doesn't touch the water and that it is straight.

PREPARATION	PRESSURIZATION	SERVINGS
20 MIN	5 MIN	6 TO 8
FREEZING	**PRESSURE COOKING**	**FREEZES**
15 MIN	32 MIN	-
COOLING	**DEPRESSURIZATION**	
5 H	10 MIN	

DOUBLE OAT OATMEAL

1 cup	**(250 ml) water**
1 cup	**(250 ml) plain oat beverage (or any other dairy-free beverage or milk)**
1 cup	**(180 g) steel-cut oats (see note)**
	Maple sugar, to taste (optional)
	Nuts, of your choice, to taste (optional)
	Fresh or dried fruit, to taste (optional)

In the container of your pressure cooker, combine the water, oat beverage and oats. Secure the lid and set to Low pressure. Set the cooking time to 12 minutes.

When ready, depressurize your pressure cooker manually, then remove the lid. Mix well and let rest for 5 minutes.

Divide the oatmeal among four bowls. Top with maple sugar, nuts and fresh or dried fruit, if desired.

NOTES *Steel-cut oats, also called Irish or Scottish oats, are hulled whole oats cut into small pieces. You can replace steel-cut oats with large flake oats—just reduce the cooking time to 5 minutes.*

The recipe doubles easily. The cooking time will remain the same.

PREPARATION	PRESSURE COOKING	SERVINGS
5 MIN	12 MIN	4

PRESSURIZATION	DEPRESSURIZATION	FREEZES
5 MIN	MANUAL	-

GIANT PANCAKE

2 cups   **(300 g) unbleached all-purpose flour**
2 tsp   **baking powder**
2   **eggs**
¼ cup   **(55 g) sugar**
1 tsp   **(5 ml) vanilla**
1¾ cups **(430 ml) milk**

Butter the container of your pressure cooker generously.

In a bowl, combine the flour and baking powder.

In another bowl, whisk together the eggs, sugar and vanilla using an electric mixer until the mixture triples in volume, about 5 minutes. With the machine running on low speed, add the dry ingredients, alternating with the milk, then mix until the batter is smooth.

Pour the batter into the container. Secure the lid and set to Low pressure. Set the cooking time to 30 minutes.

When ready, depressurize your pressure cooker manually, then remove the lid. Using oven mitts, remove the container of the pressure cooker. Place a plate upside down over the container. Flip the pancake onto the plate while it's hot. Delicious served with maple syrup, fresh blueberries or blueberry sauce (recipe p. 145).

PREPARATION	PRESSURE COOKING	SERVINGS
15 MIN	30 MIN	4 TO 6
PRESSURIZATION	**DEPRESSURIZATION**	**FREEZES**
5 MIN	MANUAL	–

BLUEBERRY SAUCE

½ cup   (125 ml) water
¼ cup   (55 g) sugar, or more to taste
2 tbsp   cornstarch
4 cups   (560 g) frozen blueberries (see note)

In a pot off the heat, whisk together the water, sugar and cornstarch. Add the blueberries. Cook over medium heat, stirring with a wooden spoon, until the sauce simmers. Continue cooking for 1 minute.

Pour into a bowl and let cool for 30 minutes. The sauce will keep for up to 1 week in an airtight container in the refrigerator. Reheat in the microwave oven, as needed.

NOTE *You can also use 1 (21 oz/600 g) bag of frozen blueberries.*

PREPARATION	COOLING	FREEZES
5 MIN	30 MIN	–
COOKING	**MAKES**	
10 MIN	3 CUPS (750 ML), APPROX.	

HARD-BOILED EGGS

6 eggs

Pour 1 ½ cups (375 ml) of water into the container of your pressure cooker. Place the silicone grill or steaming tray in the bottom, then add the eggs. Secure the lid and set to High pressure. Set the cooking time to 6 minutes for soft yolks, or 8 minutes for firmer yolks.

When ready, depressurize your pressure cooker manually, then remove the lid. Remove the eggs from the pressure cooker and place them in an ice bath to stop the cooking. Shell the eggs. Compost the egg shells.

NOTES *The biggest advantage of eggs cooked in the pressure cooker is that they peel very easily. You can cook more eggs without changing the cooking time.*

PREPARATION	PRESSURE COOKING	MAKES
5 MIN	6 MIN	6

PRESSURIZATION	DEPRESSURIZATION	FREEZES
5 MIN	MANUAL	–

ONCE COOKED,
THEY PRACTICALLY
SHELL THEMSELVES!

RICOTTA

4 cups	(1 L) 3.25% milk
¼ cup	(60 ml) lemon juice
½ tsp	fleur de sel or kosher salt
2 tbsp	(30 ml) 35% cream (optional)

Pour the milk into the container of the pressure cooker. Secure the lid and select the Yogurt function. Set the cooking time to 4 hours.

After 1 hour (the pressure cooker will beep after 1 hour of heating), remove the lid. Add the lemon juice and salt. Stir gently with a spatula for 5 seconds. Secure the lid and cook for 3 hours.

Remove the lid. Line a sieve with four layers of cheesecloth. Place the sieve over a bowl. Transfer the curd to the sieve. Drain for 15 minutes, or longer for a firmer cheese. Stir in the cream for a creamier texture. The ricotta will keep for up to 1 week in an airtight container in the refrigerator.

PREPARATION	REST	FREEZES
10 MIN	15 MIN	–

COOKING	MAKES
4 H	1 ¼ CUPS (310 ML)

INDEX BY SECTIONS

BREAKFASTS & SWEETS

INDEX BY RECIPE TYPE

DESSERTS